More Than a Coach

What It Means to Play for
Coach, Mentor, and Friend Jim Tressel

David Lee Morgan, Jr.

TRIUMPH
B O O K S

Library of Congress Cataloging-in-Publication Data

Morgan, David Lee.
    More than a coach : what it means to play for coach, mentor, and friend Jim Tressel / by David Lee Morgan Jr.
        p. cm.
    ISBN 978-1-60078-238-1
    1. Tressel, Jim. 2. Football coaches—Ohio—Biography. 3. Youngstown State University—Football—History. 4. Ohio State Buckeyes (Football team)—History. 5. Ohio State University—Football—History. I. Title.

    GV939.T68M67 2009
    796.332092—dc22
    [B]

                                                                    2009017454

This book is available in quantity at special discounts for your group or organization. For further information, contact:

Triumph Books
542 South Dearborn Street
Suite 750
Chicago, Illinois 60605
(312) 939-3330
Fax (312) 663-3557
www.triumphbooks.com

Printed in U.S.A.
ISBN: 978-1-60078-238-1

Design by Amy Flammang-Carter

Photo credits: pages 10, 18, 28, 32, 35, 44, 161 courtesy of the *Warren Tribune Chronicle*; pages 13, 14, 16, 20, 22, 29, 93, 111, 140, 174, and 176 courtesy of Trevor Parks/YSU; pages 57, 58, 66, 67, 85, 95, 98, 100, 115, 117, 128, 138, 157, 167, 181, and 186 courtesy of Gary Housteau

Contents

Foreword

The reason that we came up with the idea of *The Winner's Manual* was that when I first went to YSU, I fulfilled that dream of getting a head coaching job. I then said to myself, *OK, what is my purpose going to be as a head coach?* Obviously, I know my goal is to win games and stay employed, but what is my *purpose* going to be? And we decided as a staff, and I decided as a coach, that our purpose was going to be to help prepare men to live meaningful lives well beyond football. To plant seeds that might not sprout today, but once they are cultivated and watered and tested with the harsh weather and everything else, they are going to sprout and be strong.

And I think, too, that we thought that the more whole our program was at YSU, the more it would probably help us in football. So we went about every year adding a little bit to our *Winner's Manual*, and a little bit more, and a little bit more and a little bit more. Sometimes it's gotten a little bit too big, so we had to pare it down a bit.

Inside *The Winner's Manual* there's a section called "Fundamentals for Winners" and there are 19 fundamentals there. We've never (publicly) published *The Winner's Manual*. Every once in a while, I'll have one of my guys from the NFL give me a call or email and say, "Hey Coach Tressel, can you send me this year's *Winner's Manual*? I want to read from it."

I'd like to think that if a guy was here for three or four years, he has a couple of them still in his possession. The players keep them every year, they don't have to turn them in. And if you leave the program, we clean your locker out. I'm sure there are some guys who didn't take theirs along with them or whatever, but for the most part, I don't see them lying around.

The whole concept is the strength in the team. If you're all trying to grow in the same areas with the same *Winner's Manual* fundamentals, you're growing together. And I think, too, that the thing we knew at YSU was that very few guys were going to make football their career. So with that in mind, *The Winner's Manual* at YSU was important. But even here, though, at The Ohio State University, not too many of our guys are going to play more than five years in the NFL. So, OK, they are in their late twenties and now they have to face life.

I think it's a difficult challenge when someone has gone from about age eight through 28 as the star and everyone has been applauding him and everyone has wanted him on their team. Then all of a sudden he is 28 and no one cares how fast he can run anymore.

Hopefully by that time, some of those seeds have sprouted. You know, the seeds that really have nothing to do with football, but they have everything to do with football.

— Jim Tressel

Author's Note

I can honestly say without question that in my 20-plus-year career in journalism, this book is the most important project I've ever completed. It means more to me than anything I've ever written.

What makes it so important is not just what Coach Tressel means to me, but what he means to everyone from his former and current players at Youngstown State and Ohio State to anyone else who has had the honor and privilege of getting to know him over the years.

I first met Coach Tressel in 1986, when I was a sophomore at Youngstown State. I never played for Coach Tressel, but all my roommates were football players and they did. I walked on at YSU as a baseball player in '85 and '86, but immature decisions shortened my career. But because my roommates were football players, I was acquainted with Coach Tressel as well as his coaching philosophies on and off the field.

My roommates were always reading and talking about this book that they had. So one day, I went into one of my roommates' rooms, picked it up, and started leafing through it. The next thing I knew, hours had gone by. I was completely captivated by the book. I remember I had to go to class, so I put the book back. I went to class walking on air, feeling like I was a Rhodes Scholar, like I could run for president, that I could cure cancer. I felt I could do whatever I put my mind to.

I found out later that the book is called *The Winner's Manual*. It's basically a 300-page handbook that Coach Tressel hands out to his players when they report to preseason camp in August. The first part of the book deals with the team's preseason schedule, general policies and procedures, and other items pertaining to the program. Then, tucked back more than 200 pages into the book is a section called "Fundamentals for Winners." The fundamentals are basic elements of life that can help anyone become a better person regardless of what they do in life.

There are 19 fundamentals in *The Winner's Manual*: attitude, caring, class, discipline, enthusiasm, excellence, faith/belief, focus, gratitude, handling adversity, heroes/winners, hope, humility, love, persistence, responsibility, team, toughness, and work. Each section is composed of inspirational quotes, short stories, and anecdotes to illustrate each fundamental. Tressel started handing out *The Winner's Manual* in his first year at YSU in 1986, and he continues to do it with his players at Ohio State.

A few years ago, I was in Columbus covering the state high school track and field championships. We had a break between events, so I thought to myself, *I wonder if Coach Tressel is at the Woody Hayes Complex*. I walked over to his office, and his secretary, Deb, an absolutely wonderful lady, was there. She told me Coach Tressel was in a meeting, so I figured I would catch him another time. As I was walking out, Coach Tressel was coming out of a meeting room down the hall with assistant coaches Mel Tucker and Luke Fickell. He did a double-take and yelled, "David, is that you?" I told him I was in town on assignment.

He said, "C'mon down here, let me introduce you to some of my coaches."

A few minutes later, he said, "How much time do you have?"

I told him I had about an hour before the competition resumed.

"Then, let me take you on an official tour around the complex," he said proudly.

He showed me everything—the equipment room, weight room, video room, the indoor football facility. Afterward, we went into his office and we reminisced about Youngstown and how we both had come a long way. He told me how proud he was to see me doing well. I asked him if I could get a copy of that year's *Winner's Manual*. He didn't hesitate to send me off with one.

Years later, I contacted him about writing a book on *The Winner's Manual* and its importance in his life. He invited me to Columbus to talk more about it. I put together a proposal and explained to him how I would write a book based on stories from former players and coaches from Youngstown State and Ohio State, and even some current Ohio State players, about how *The Winner's Manual* has positively influenced them on and off the field. I would also talk to other people he has inspired. Coach Tressel liked the idea and he graciously agreed to let me write the book and to contribute a foreword.

My hope is that this book will do for you as a reader what *The Winner's Manual* has done for me and for hundreds of Coach Tressel's players over the years: inspire you to be the best you can be, in everything you do.

1 The Perfect Season

14-0. It had never been done until 2002. And the Buckeyes—
or "Luckeyes," as many Ohio State critics labeled them
because of the team's numerous last-second wins that season—faced a
difficult challenge heading into the 2002 Tostitos Fiesta Bowl national
championship game against the Miami Hurricanes.

The Buckeyes won six of their 13 regular-season games by seven
points or less: Cincinnati (23–19), Wisconsin (19–14), Penn State (13–7),
Purdue (10–6), Illinois (23–16), and Michigan (14–9). Miami, led
by Heisman Trophy candidate and quarterback Ken Dorsey, tight
end Kellen Winslow (who later became NFL teammates with the
Cleveland Browns), and running back Willis McGahee, who would
go on to be a star running back for the Buffalo Bills, had dismantled their opponents all season. Going into the Fiesta Bowl, the
Hurricanes boasted the nation's longest Division I-A winning streak
at 34 games.

To say that Ohio State was an underdog coming into the game
was an understatement of epic proportions. The Ohio-State-Has-No-
Chance-of-Beating-the-Mighty-Hurricanes Express started gaining
momentum as soon as the matchup was announced. During press
conferences days before the game, Ohio State quarterback Craig
Krenzel, the Buckeyes' steady leader, was asked how his team would
react if it fell behind early by two touchdowns, even three.

"We don't plan on it happening to have to worry about it. You
know, at the same time if it does happen, I don't think we will change
our game plan," Krenzel said. "We will stick to what works, and we

know that if your defense does give up a couple of quick scores that they're going to change as well. If they come out and get 21 points on us real quick, we have the confidence to come back and get those points back during the course of the game. Obviously, unless it's in the fourth quarter. If we're down in the second quarter, we understand there is a whole other half to play to score."

And Krenzel had demonstrated all season long that he could rally his team back from a deficit. "Having played in many close games, we know how to keep our composure and keep our focus on the game and to go out to make the plays to win," he said. "Personally, that's just kind of the way I've always been. I've always been laid back and calm regardless of the situation."

Krenzel was never the type of player to be overconfident, but he was confident in his team's ability to play with Miami. "Going into the national championship was really no different than any other [game]," Krenzel said. "We were supremely confident in our ability as a team and confident that we could go out and win, regardless of what anyone else was saying. But going into that game, it wasn't different than the others. It was business as usual. We knew what it took to win. The coaching staff knew what it took to win. We felt very prepared and, beyond that, we knew it was going to be up to execution. We knew it was going to be a roller coaster of a game. Very few football games follow through the whole way you expect because there's so many ups and downs and that's just part of the game."

> "Going into that game, it wasn't different than the others. It was business as usual. We knew what it took to win."
>
> —OSU quarterback Craig Krenzel

Confidence wasn't something freshman running back Maurice Clarett lacked; it was and always had been his style. He wasn't the type of player who would hold back his feelings, as he showed several times during the course of the season, such as the time he got into an altercation with running backs coach Tim Spencer on the sidelines earlier that season. Clarett's feeling about the Hurricanes was, *Who are they?* He felt that the Buckeyes were just as good as Miami and had earned the right to be playing for the title, even though odds-makers made Miami the overwhelming favorite.

"I kind of like being an underdog," Clarett said during interviews leading up to the game. "You have nothing to lose and everything to gain. It gives you more incentive to fight [harder] on every play." He was asked if he was concerned about Miami. In typical Clarett fashion, he wasn't about to give in to anything. "You don't go 'wow,'" he said. "Everybody puts their pants on the same way. Anything can happen that day. I mean, we just have a game plan. I hope we stick to our game plan and worry about ourselves."

The rest of the Ohio State team and coaching staff felt the same way as Clarett when they talked about the confidence they had in Krenzel. As talented as Ohio State's defense was—with the likes of All-American safety Mike Doss, All-American linebacker Matt Wilhelm, All–Big Ten defensive back Chris Gamble and All–Big Ten defensive linemen Darrion Scott and Kenny Peterson—Krenzel still was the player who held the keys to whether Ohio State would prevail.

"He's really tough," offensive lineman Shane Olivea said about Krenzel. "This year he's been able to show that he's able to do what he's been able to do.... He's someone you want to have in that huddle, fourth-and-1. There is no one else I want throwing that ball." Then Clarett quickly added: "I would be in the huddle, nervous, and you look at Craig and he gives you more confidence. So he's not worried about it, so why should I be? I hope he can keep his composure through January 3."

Krenzel was at Ohio State from 1999 to 2003 and made his big splash when he took over for suspended quarterback Steve Bellisari late in the 2001 season. Krenzel's first start for the Buckeyes was at

Michigan, his home state (he is from Utica), and he led the Buckeyes to their first win against Michigan in Ann Arbor since 1987, 26–20.

And on January 3, 2002, Krenzel helped Ohio State make history, with that stunning 31–24 double-overtime win against Miami and Ohio State's first national championship since 1968. The game was an instant classic, one of the most thrilling college national football championships in history. Besides taking the national championship, Ohio State became the first Division I football team in history to win 14 games.

There were so many big plays for both teams, but for Ohio State, none was bigger than the pass interference call the Buckeyes received on fourth down and trailing by a touchdown in the first overtime. Krenzel attempted a pass to Chris Gamble in the end zone. It fell incomplete, and Miami players and fans started to celebrate—a little too prematurely—as an official threw a late flag for pass interference on the Hurricanes. Even Coach Tressel felt it was over.

"I thought that there was interference but I did not see a flag for a moment," Tressel said. "I thought, *Isn't that a shame*, because I think the ball was thrown well…. Craig came up with the thought on the play for Chris to do the route he did. I thought he [was] interfered with. I didn't see a flag. You know we don't complain about things if they don't go our way. It was good to see that guy come up in the back of the end zone and make what I thought was a good call."

Krenzel's account?

"You know, after I threw that, I got hit," Krenzel said. "As I was getting hit, the ball was in the air and I saw contact going on in the corner. The ball fell incomplete and their team rushed the field, and I sat there. And to be honest, it was a feeling of dejection, thinking the game was over, knowing how hard we played and how much effort we put in, and just at that time thinking we weren't victorious. I thought there was contact, but I didn't see the flag until after I got up. I think it was the right call."

To understand how special that season was for Ohio State, one must consider the countless situations where the Buckeyes' backs were against the wall and the only way to succeed was to focus on the task at hand, one of Tressel's favorite sayings.

Earlier in the season, Ohio State was down 6–3 on the road against Purdue. It was late in the game and they were facing fourth-and-1. Tressel could have sent in place kicker Mike Nugent to attempt a 54-yard field goal to tie the game. He could have tried running the ball for the first down. Instead, he called King Right 64 Y Shallow Swap, and Krenzel hit wide receiver Michael Jenkins in the corner of the end zone for a 37-yard touchdown strike.

"Holy Buckeye," were the words that came from famed ABC announcer Brent Musberger.

"Michael Jenkins ran a go route and I'm pretty sure Coach Tressel was probably surprised I threw the ball there, too," Krenzel said with a chuckle. "There were a number of underneath options, more short to intermediate routes that we were really calling to just get the first down. The defensive look that they gave us, I knew what they were trying to do, our guys up front protected well and I knew I had Michael one-on-one on the outside. Regardless of the situation, that's a matchup that you just can't pass up. I went through my progressions and just felt the best place to go with the ball was to Mike, and it worked out because of the focus every one of my teammates had on that play. Our focus that entire season was extraordinary and you saw the end result: an undefeated season and an undisputed national championship."

The poise and character Krenzel and the 2002 team showed trickled down to the younger players, like defensive back Nate Salley, who was a role player at the time. Salley was a safety at Ohio State from 2002 to 2005 and became one of the hardest-hitting defensive backs in the Big Ten. He was a fourth-round pick of the Carolina Panthers in the 2006 NFL draft.

"My freshman year was a crazy season because we won so many close games that went down to the last minute," Salley said. "And when it came to big games or any game, period, you always knew where Coach Tressel was going to come from. He continually preached that no matter what, no matter the situation, always believe in yourself. He never let us not believe in ourselves, he never let us get to that point. We felt like it was our year. We had gone through so much that year with all of those close games and we hadn't given up the whole season. We had been through some crazy games against Illinois, Purdue, and Cincinnati, but we always found a way to win. You don't ever give up on yourself. You never give up on your teammates and you always believe in one another. When you do that, you'll always find a way to get through tough times. It doesn't mean you'll always find a way to win, but you'll always find a way to get through those tough times."

Simon Fraser was a defensive lineman for the Buckeyes from 2001 to 2004 and an exceptional player in his time at Ohio State. He epitomized the term "student-athlete." He was a key member of that 2002 national championship team, but more impressive was that he was a three-time scholar-athlete at Ohio State and earned academic All–Big Ten conference honors twice.

Now a player in the NFL, he never tires of talking about "the Game."

"During that national championship game, we all understood what the game meant," Fraser said. "The biggest thing that stood out to me was when Coach Tressel looked around the locker room and said, 'Everybody out there in America is against us and no one thinks we have a chance playing this game tonight. But as long as all of us in this room stick together and hang by each other's side, we can go out there and win this game.' That's basically the mentality we had. We believed that we could get it done, and through the experiences that we had during the season, we knew we could overcome any obstacles or any situations that we were going to face."

It took Tressel just two seasons to do what no other Ohio State football coach had done in 34 years, and that was bring a national championship to Columbus. "You know, it will be something that will be very, very special the rest of their lives," Tressel said of the national championship. "They did it 100 percent with great faith and belief in what we were trying to accomplish."

Tressel's longtime friend Dr. John Geletka had always believed in Tressel, going back to their days in Youngstown. Geletka, who is also Tressel's agent, knew no one expected Ohio State to even challenge for a national championship that year, given the fact that the Buckeyes finished 7–5 the previous season, Tressel's first year. There were skeptics who questioned why a storied program such as Ohio State even hired Tressel, who had come from Division I-AA Youngstown State. This was a man with no Division I head coaching experience, and now he was leading one of the most successful Division I programs in the country! None of that mattered, though. Tressel, his players, and his supporters all believed in each other.

"When you look at that 2002 national championship season at Ohio State, and you look at the players he had that season, it's an amazing thing for them to have even made it that far," Geletka said. "There wasn't a superstar on that team. You had a lot of players that worked together to get to where they wanted to be and Jim always convinced them that they could get to the national championship game. If you watched Jim during the championship game, his demeanor never changed. And if you watched him during the other close games that season, he was the same way. If he was up by 24 points or down by 24 points, his demeanor never changed on the sideline. He was always calm, cool, and collected. But when they won the national championship against Miami, I was just overwhelmed."

Krenzel was named the Offensive Most Valuable Player of the national championship game, posted a 24–3 overall record as a starter, was a three-time All–Big Ten award winner, and won a host of postseason national awards. "All I know is Krenzel did for us what we needed done," Tressel said. "He led the team, fought like crazy, he made plays, most especially when they had to be made. He's tough. Probably the number one characteristic that a quarterback better have, especially a quarterback at Ohio State—he better be tough. Craig was tough. He played tough."

But the biggest accomplishment for Krenzel during his college career was earning his degree in molecular genetics from The Ohio State University soon afterward.

2 The State of Youngstown: Where It All Began

Youngstown, Ohio: a burg in northeastern Ohio with a population of 82,026, halfway between New York and Chicago, and equidistant from Cleveland and Pittsburgh. It is a city known for its steel mills, with an eclectic mix of immigrants—African American, Greek, Hispanic, Slovakian, and many others. It is a population that cares about working hard, earning a decent living, and raising their families to be God-fearing, proud Americans. These are people who are proud to call the Mahoning Valley home.

A casualty of the collapse of the prosperous steel mills in the late '70s and early '80s, the people of Youngstown found their city blighted by drugs, organized crime, and unprecedented unemployment rates. But what proud Mahoning Valley residents still had was their sports, specifically, their high school football. Youngstown Cardinal Mooney, Youngstown Ursuline, Warren Harding, Farrell, Canfield, Girard, Lakeview, Niles, Campbell, Struthers, Lowellville, Chaney, Woodrow Wilson. Those were big names in high school football, and fans packed the stadiums on Friday nights. There was a modest turnout for the team at the local university, Youngstown State, but Youngstown was a Friday night town.

Then, in 1986, a new sheriff rolled into town, and his name was Jim Tressel. He was a 33-year-old quarterbacks coach at Ohio State under Buckeyes head coach Earle Bruce when he was hired to replace former longtime YSU coach Bill Narduzzi, who had been the coach from 1975 to 1985 for a 68–51–1 record.

He might have looked more like an '80s game show host than a head football coach, but Tressel knew how to win it all in the "Showcase Showdown": the Division I-AA national championship.

When the YSU job opened, Dr. John Geletka made the phone call to Columbus.

"I was on the Board of Trustees and chaired the committee that selected him," said Geletka, a successful dentist in Youngstown who was also a sports agent. He eventually became Tressel's agent and the two became close friends. "The first thing I did during the process was call Earle Bruce. I said, 'Coach Bruce, we're looking for a coach at Youngstown State. Is there anybody on your staff that you would recommend for this job?' Coach Bruce then replied, 'That job is a diamond-in-the-rough and there are two guys I can recommend.'"

The two coaches Bruce recommended were (future Minnesota head coach) Glen Mason and Tressel. Mason expressed no interest in the YSU job, but Tressel went up for an interview.

Bruce remembered Tressel being somewhat reluctant to even apply for the job. "When Jim was on my staff at Ohio State, I knew he had a chance to become the head coach at Youngstown State and I told him, 'You go get that job because you'll make that a great football job.' They were dying for a winner up there at Youngstown State and they had great football players. But Jim told me he wanted to be a coach at a small school like his dad, Lee Tressel [who had coached at Baldwin-Wallace], for the rest of his life."

"We had two interviews with potential candidates before Jim and two more after him," Geletka said. "But after we interviewed Jim, I told our athletic director [Joe Malmisur], 'We're done. Cancel the other interviews. This is the guy we're going to hire.'"

Malmisur admitted Tressel wasn't his first choice. "My number one choice was Jim Gruden, the father of [Tampa Bay Buccaneers head coach] Jon Gruden. Jim Gruden was an offensive coach at Notre Dame and he was the one I definitely wanted."

But Tressel got the job after a tremendous interview, Malmisur said. "The thing I find amusing is how members of the press sort of belittled the fact that Tressel emphasized the family concept. He wasn't received with open arms," Malmisur said.

Geletka was impressed by Tressel's demeanor. He remembered that Tressel did not have one note in front of him when he interviewed for the job.

The year before Tressel arrived at YSU, the Penguins, who played in the Ohio Valley Conference, were 5–6. The program was in turmoil and it was apparent that Narduzzi was on his way out.

The first step in the Tressel era was to look for a model to follow. "When we came to Youngstown State as a staff, there were a couple of programs we focused on and one was Eastern Kentucky," Tressel said. The Colonels, led by legendary coach Roy Kidd, were the dominant Division I-AA team at the time. They had played in four national championship games, and had won two, when Tressel took the reins at YSU in 1986.

"We felt like we had to get as good as Eastern Kentucky if we ever were going to get to the top," Tressel said. "And just at that point, Georgia Southern had emerged as a premier program. They had won [Division I-AA] championships in the mid '80s and [later] in the '90s. I remember being on a recruiting trip with Jim Bollman, driving through Virginia, and we stopped at a pay phone. I called back to the office and Joe Malmisur told me that we were looking for games because we got nudged out of the [Ohio Valley Conference] when Akron left. Joe said the only teams he could find that had games for an independent team were Georgia Southern and Stephen F. Austin, and SFA had just played for a national championship. So I said, 'Well, let's sign them both up.' Joe told me I was crazy."

All of the players weren't sold on the 33-year-old Tressel right away. Though they complained about Narduzzi's old-school and somewhat out-of-touch coaching philosophies, they loved and revered him. He could be extremely hard at times, but off the field he had a heart of gold. It didn't matter who was taking over for Narduzzi—it could have been the Gipper himself—there would have been considerable animosity toward the new coach.

One of the players who was skeptical of this young new coach was Vince Peterson. A defensive lineman from YSU from 1983–1986, Peterson was the oldest of three boys and grew up in nearby Warren, Ohio, home of Pro Football Hall of Famer Paul Warfield, the late and former Ohio State and Minnesota Vikings All-Pro offensive lineman Korey Stringer, and the infamous Maurice Clarett. Peterson learned from his parents the importance of hard work and being a man of high character. Peterson remains one of Tressel's favorite players to this day. But it was a bond that took a while to develop.

Peterson was a senior when Tressel arrived on the scene and the coach counted on him to be a team leader. "We were hearing a lot of big name coaches [were] coming in to interview and one of them was Gerry Faust," Peterson recalled. "Faust was fresh from Notre Dame—obviously a big-time program—and the players felt he would bring a lot of notoriety to YSU. So a lot of us, to tell you the truth, were looking for Faust to come in."

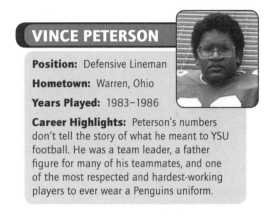

VINCE PETERSON

Position: Defensive Lineman

Hometown: Warren, Ohio

Years Played: 1983–1986

Career Highlights: Peterson's numbers don't tell the story of what he meant to YSU football. He was a team leader, a father figure for many of his teammates, and one of the most respected and hardest-working players to ever wear a Penguins uniform.

Geletka confirmed that Faust was on a short list, so to speak. He recalled watching the Miami Hurricanes play Notre Dame in the last game of the 1985 season, and that Notre Dame coach Faust had already announced his resignation at the end of the season.

Geletka was a shrewd businessman, and he wanted to get his school some notoriety. "We needed some national exposure," he said. "So I called the sports information director at Miami at the time [Rich Dalrymple] and said, 'Rich, I want to talk to Gerry Faust. Could you leave him a note about our job at Youngstown State?'"

That was the morning of Notre Dame's game at the Orange Bowl against Miami and Geletka received a call from Faust. "I answered and said, 'Coach, we're looking for a head coach. I'd like to have you come up and take a look around at our school and the facilities.' Gerry was in Youngstown the next morning. We took him on a tour of the facility. I wanted him there not so much to hire him, but [because] we wanted some national publicity. That's how Gerry Faust came to Youngstown State from Notre Dame, to look at the job opening. He came up and loved it and thought it would be a great fit for him."

The University of Akron was YSU's rival, and Geletka hinted that athletic administrators at Akron became so concerned that Faust was going to Youngstown that that they hired him themselves two days later.

"He hadn't even started our interview process," Geletka said. "In my personal opinion, that's how Faust got the Akron job."

Meanwhile, Peterson said when he and his teammates heard that Tressel was the leading candidate and would more than likely get the job, they weren't happy. "We were all like, 'Who the heck is Jim Tressel?'

"I remember going into spring ball my senior year and Coach Tressel had us running from Stambaugh Stadium down through Wick Park, and up and down Fifth Avenue. He actually ran it with us and it was about three miles. That's all I was good for anyway. But Coach Tressel running with us got my attention, and I realized that he really was all about bringing us together as a team, like he talked about when he first addressed the team after he was hired.

"I remember my dad always telling me and my younger brothers not to ever lead someone into doing something that you wouldn't do yourself. So that was one of the first things that caught my attention about Coach Tressel. He wouldn't tell us to do something if he wouldn't do it himself."

MIKE PETERSON

Position: Linebacker
Hometown: Warren, Ohio
Years Played: 1984-1987
Career Highlights: Peterson was a captain for Tressel his senior year and helped lead YSU to an 8-4 record and a 5-1 record in the Ohio Valley Conference. He was a second-team all-OVC selection in 1987.

Vince Peterson had a younger brother, Michael, who had also played for Narduzzi. Michael Peterson was a linebacker for YSU from 1984 to 1988, and was an outstanding Division I recruit who had offers from schools like Michigan State and

Iowa State. But family meant the most to Michael, so he followed in his older brother Vince's footsteps. Vince was by that point a team leader at Youngstown State and Mike wanted the opportunity to play college football with his brother. In fact, there were three Peterson brothers who played for Tressel at the same time. Andre Peterson, the youngest brother, was also an outstanding linebacker for the Penguins.

> *"Coach Tressel looked at me and said, 'Michael, didn't your mother just tell you to eat your salad?'"*

Michael Peterson was skeptical of Tressel as well. "When I signed with Youngstown State, it was the only Division I-AA school that even talked to me. Everyone else thought I was going to a Division I school," Michael Peterson said. "I had narrowed down my choices to Michigan State, Iowa State, and Purdue. Part of the reason I chose YSU was that we have a close-knit family. My brother was a starter there at the time and the fact that my father would get to see me play was a big piece, as well.

"I'll be frank, I wasn't all that happy with going to YSU at first," Mike admitted. "The first time I sat down and actually talked to Coach Tressel was when we were at a football awards banquet and I was getting some kind of football award. I was sitting at a table with my mom and dad, and Coach Tressel was there sitting with us. We were getting ready to eat dinner and my mother just looked over at me and said, 'You know, Michael, you really need to learn to eat salad.' I looked at her and said, 'Ma, you know I don't eat salad.' Coach Tressel looked at me and said, 'Michael, didn't your mother just tell you to eat your salad?' Well, of course I ate it and I was peeved and I thought, *This isn't going to work, me playing for this guy.* But right there, Coach Tressel set the tone for how he was going to run his program."

Michael maintains a close friendship with Tressel to this day.

It wasn't just football players whom Tressel impacted. Everyone associated with the program instantly saw something unique in

Tressel's approach to the game, and perhaps more importantly, his approach to people.

At Youngstown State, his relationship with quarterback Trenton Lykes was more than that of just coach and player. It was coach, mentor, and friend. Lykes, who left YSU and became a lieutenant colonel in the United States Air Force, was responsible for laying the groundwork for the success Youngstown State experienced in the '90s. He was Tressel's quarterback for two seasons and he helped slowly move the Penguins into the upper echelon of the Division I-AA ranks. Lykes mirrored Tressel in many ways. He was meticulous about details and a proven leader. He was in the ROTC program at YSU and routinely wore his uniform to the weekly press conferences.

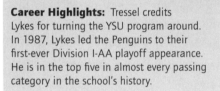

TRENTON LYKES

Position: Quarterback

Hometown: Akron, Ohio

Years Played: 1984–1987

Career Highlights: Tressel credits Lykes for turning the YSU program around. In 1987, Lykes led the Penguins to their first-ever Division I-AA playoff appearance. He is in the top five in almost every passing category in the school's history.

Lykes was inducted into the YSU Hall of Fame in 1997. "Trenton is simply the man that gave this program direction," Tressel said. "He paved the way for our 1-AA playoff success. If it were not for Trenton, I might be teaching and coaching at a junior high school somewhere."

Lykes was named the Ohio Valley Conference Offensive Player of the Year his senior year in 1987. "I owe all of my success and records to Coach Tressel," said Lykes, who graduated from Akron (Ohio) Firestone High School, the same high school that produced model and actress Angie Everhart, Chrissie Hynde of The Pretenders, actress Melina Kanakaredes, astronaut Judith Resnik, 2004 Olympic gold medalist swimmer Mark Gangloff, and Chris Ash, two-time Olympic swimming trials participant.

"When Coach Tressel came here my junior year, he actually taught me how to be a quarterback. No one else ever did that. And to me, it was like being reborn. It was like one of those life-altering moments."

In one of the first quarterback meetings Lykes had with Tressel in the spring of his junior year, Tressel never talked about offense. Instead, he began to teach Lykes how to read defenses. "No one had ever approached it that way for me," Lykes said. "It felt like a rebirth for me as a quarterback. My understanding of the position just multiplied. Before Coach Tressel came in, there weren't a lot of people high on me. At the time, Bob Courtney and I were still going back and forth at the starting position. But when Coach Tressel arrived, that was about the first time in my life in just about doing anything that I felt prepared. I mean, I knew what was going to happen before it was going to happen. If I would've had that man [as my head coach] for four years, there's no telling what I could've accomplished."

Lykes, who used to be nervous on the field in the past, never played nervously again. Sure, he had the pre-game butterflies, but after kick-off he was confident and in control. He remembered games where the defense would fake a blitz and he would look at the safety and the linebacker and just smile because he knew they weren't blitzing. It was because of the preparation and confidence Tressel gave him. He knew what was going to happen before it happened and it relaxed him and allowed his athleticism and leadership qualities to shine.

"The other thing I can tell you is that Coach Tressel was the first person—and I'm being sincere about this—who *verbally* gave me confidence," Lykes said. "Even though I played football practically my entire life, he gave me confidence I never had before. I remember when he told me I was going to be the starting quarterback my senior year, and I remember him telling me that I could be an all-conference quarterback. He was the first person that ever told me, 'I think you're pretty good.' And at that time in my life, I was like, 'Huh? I am?' I

As an always-insightful coach, Tressel was the ultimate storyteller and motivator for his players at Youngstown State, and later at Ohio State.

didn't think I was a *bad* quarterback, but I never thought of myself as being all-conference. I never did. Like the records I set or broke, I never thought in my life I would do any of those things. My only goal was to be a quarterback and start. That was it. And when I was inducted into the YSU Hall of Fame, it never crossed my mind that it would ever happen.

"Going into my senior year, Coach Tressel sat me down and showed me all the school records I had broken and, again, I was shocked. Because I wasn't keeping up with that kind of stuff. Then, he told me I could break Phil Simms' conference passing record because Simms played at Morehead State. I never thought about myself in that light, as far as being a record-setting quarterback, until Coach Tressel instilled that confidence and belief in myself."

Tressel allowed Lykes to change plays at the line of scrimmage, something Lykes had never done before. (And if it was a bad audible, Lykes was never, ever scolded.) Instead, they talked about what would have been the best play to call, came to an agreement, then moved on. They were in sync; Tressel allowed Lykes to go out and execute Tressel's game plan with a free rein.

Tressel felt blessed to have a quarterback like Lykes. "Trenton was coming into his junior year when he first played for me and there had been some ups and downs, some wins and losses, and some questions about who was going to be the quarterback," Tressel said. "Sometimes, it's good for a player when there's a coaching staff transition and other times it's not as good. But the timing was right for Trenton because he had all the tools you could possibly have, but what I thought he had was the character and leadership ability and that great trait of being grateful. Whenever you're grateful for something, you have a better chance of having the right attitude and he had the perfect attitude.

"That first year, we weren't a good team by any means but Trenton was grateful for the confidence that everyone had in him and he just grew and grew and grew," Tressel said. "He had the right attitude and it rubbed off on the rest of the guys, and he had the right attitude because he was grateful."

Lykes' senior year in 1987 was the first time in school history that YSU went to the Division I-AA playoffs. The Penguins lost in the last seconds to Northern Iowa at the UNI-Dome; Northern Iowa was ranked in the top five at the time. Afterward, Lykes said he felt that YSU may have been "just happy to get into the playoffs." The next week, when players were in the locker room, Tressel had a chalkboard inside with goals the players set at the beginning of the season. The only goal the players wrote on that board was to win the Ohio Valley Conference championship. "The thing Coach Tressel talked about was that we set our goals too low," Lykes said. "We did not set high expectations for ourselves. Here we are, we made it to the playoffs, which was never really a goal and we almost beat the No. 3 team in the nation."

While Lykes and Tressel sat together in the locker room, the thing that hit them both was that they underestimated themselves as a team. "I now set my goals high in everything I do," Lykes said.

During Lykes' senior year, Tressel was big on bringing in motivational speakers, from former and current athletes to businesspeople anyone with an inspirational story to share. One speaker told a story about pedaling a bike downhill. "He explained that you may pedal hard in a race and most folks, when they get to the top of the hill, they'll coast down the hill," Lykes said. "But his point was if you continue to pedal hard during the times that you're supposed to coast, then you're going to go farther than the next guy. That's another thing that always stayed with me. I always try to work harder than the next person. When they are taking a break, I continue to work."

As players got to know and understand Tressel's unconventional yet extremely effective strategies to motivate and bring his players together, Ron Strollo, a former YSU tight end from 1988 to 1991, said the summer heading into his senior year, Tressel had another novel idea to bring the team together. Tressel had his seniors gather at Stambaugh Stadium, YSU's home field. There were several white minivans lined up in a row outside the stadium. The players and coaching staff all got in the vans and they were driven to Tressel's house in Boardman for a summer barbeque. They all played basketball, ate steaks, and basically had a good time.

RON STROLLO

Position: Tight End

Hometown: Austintown, Ohio

Career Highlights: Strollo was a captain on the school's first-ever Division I-AA national championship team. He was named YSU's athletic director after Tressel moved to Ohio State, a position he still holds.

Hours later, just before dusk, they all got back into the vans. Instead of going back to campus, the vans took the players to a Boy Scout camping ground.

"We walked into the campground and everybody was thinking, *What is going on?*" Strollo said. "This ROTC guy was there and he handed us tents as we got off the van, one by one. We went out into the woods and set our tents up, then we walked down to the pavilion area and we went through about a two- or three-hour seminar on leadership."

Following that seminar, the players were told that they could all walk and find their way home or they could go back up to where their tents were pitched, spend the night, and they would be picked up the next morning.

"A majority of the guys walked up to the main road and called for rides back," Strollo said. "I stayed, and there were probably only five or six of us that stayed. The next morning, Coach Tressel came and picked us up. He was trying to teach us a lesson about being a team. He told us the story of how he was up on the street parked in his car with the lights off where no one could see and he was watching guys walk to the nearest gas station to call for someone to pick them up.

"More than anything, that got us closer to the rest of the seniors," Strollo said. "We were able to laugh more at each other and we had a great season. We went on to win the first Division I-AA national championship at YSU. We communicated with each other. It got people caring about each other, and you care about each other when you know more about each other. In '91, when we won the national championship, we won our last eight games and they were all nail-biters. But I have to say that because we all cared about each other and we were so in tune with each other, we were able to overcome all obstacles because we knew we were all playing for each other. No one was going to give up or give less than 110 percent."

Archie Herring, a YSU running back from 1987 to 1990, was a player who always did what he could to show his leadership. "When I was a senior and the younger players were coming in, I said to Coach Tressel, 'Hey coach, we have all of these young players coming in. Why don't we mentor them? I'll take the young tailbacks and they can hang with me during two-a-days.' The senior quarterback would have the freshman quarterbacks and so on. That started back at YSU and I'm sure Coach Tressel still does that now. He thought that was a great idea because it focused around the team concept."

There also was a time during Herring's senior year when the team concept was tested. There was a conflict among team members that escalated into a fight at a popular campus bar, Pal Joey's. "It was crazy," said Herring, who always kept himself out of trouble. "I think there was a small faction where there was some racial tension among a group of guys," said Herring. "I wasn't involved, but I heard about it. Me and Pete Rekstis, who later became the defensive coordinator at Kent State in 2004, laid it out to all the players in a private team meeting. We told everyone that we weren't going to have any of that nonsense. It wasn't going to be part of our family, and in order for us to be successful and do what we want to do as a family, we had to come together as a team."

ARCHIE HERRING

Position: Running Back
Hometown: Massillon, Ohio
Years Played: 1987–1990
Career Highlights: Herring started out as a defensive back, but Tressel moved him to running back, where he flourished. He finished third in school history in career all-purpose yards with 4,341. He is Youngstown State's all-time leader in kickoff returns (86) and career kickoff return yards (2,156).

After Herring and Rekstis showed admirable senior leadership by bringing the team together in diplomatic fashion, most of the players fell in line. The ones who didn't left the team. That year, 1990, YSU finished with an 11–0 regular season record. It was an incredible ride during the regular season, but it came to a heartbreaking end in the first round of the playoffs. The Penguins, who looked to be one of the favorites to possibly reach the national championship game, lost at home to Central Florida, 20–17, on a field goal with no time remaining.

"It was strange because before that game I had a premonition," Herring said. "We were all at pregame meal, sitting together at a table as a team. I pulled Coach aside and said, 'Coach Tressel, this feels kind of weird. This could be my last meal with the team.' Coach Tressel said, "It possibly could be. That's why you have to give everything you have right now. Lay it out on the field and whatever happens, happens. Just do your best."

YSU lost, and Herring and several other teammates cried as they walked off the field. There was a lot of disappointment in the locker room because YSU finished the regular season undefeated and there was so much more that the team wanted to accomplish. Then, during that extreme moment of disappointment, Herring said he understood his journey with Tressel at YSU. "It just hit me," Herring said. "I knew my career was officially over. But at the same time, I knew that it was only a game. I knew I had something to look forward to because not only did Coach Tressel prepare us for football, he prepared every single one of his players for *life*. I was lucky because I was under Coach Tressel for five years, so I knew there was going to be a tomorrow after football. We all did. Well, most of us did because Coach Tressel prepared you for that day.

"I knew that there was going to be a job, some income, some success, and an opportunity for me to make a positive impact on the community," Herring said. "So that was my comfort. Yeah, I was hurt that we lost the game, but knowing that I had something to look forward to and knowing that Coach Tressel was even going to help me if I needed it was an extraordinarily comforting feeling."

One didn't have to play for Tressel to be inspired by his philosophies on life. Kelly Palmer was a YSU cheerleader from 1983 to 1988. She was a sophomore during Tressel's first year at YSU and just being around him and the program for two seasons profoundly impacted her for the rest of her life.

"I was there at YSU during the transition from one head coach in Bill Narduzzi, who had been there a long time, into the Jim Tressel era, and the biggest thing I remember was that Coach Tressel brought a whole new vibe to Youngstown State that wasn't there— and not just with the football program, but with the entire community," Palmer said. "He brought a positive energy and a gentleman's approach to the game of football and college life in general. I saw such a huge change in a lot of the players whom I knew and met as freshmen." The truth was, Tressel changed everyone's perceptions of the football program. Palmer said that most of the players she knew before Tressel's arrival were there just for sports. Undeniably, it is a phenomenon that happens at schools all over the country. Palmer said Tressel gave the program an immediate facelift. "I saw so many of my friends who were there at YSU just to play football end up leaving with their degrees because of Coach Tressel. And to this day, they've turned out to be true gentlemen in the true sense of the word."

Palmer also acknowledged there was a certain stereotype associated with cheerleaders and that Tressel helped erase that stereotype. What it came down to was a sense of inclusion. She felt that Coach Tressel made her and her fellow cheerleaders feel special.

"Before Coach Tressel got there, we really weren't included in too much of anything as it related to the football program. We just showed up and cheered," she said. "But when Coach Tressel came, he made us part of the football family. We did office things for him. We did more than just show up in a skirt and cheer. I'll never forget when we won the Ohio Valley Conference championship in 1987. He got all the cheerleaders championship watches. It was such a great gesture and it made us feel like we were part of the football family. Yet, you could be John Doe, student number 1,999, and Coach

Tressel had this magnetic personality that could make you feel like you wanted to play football, even if you never played it before or you hated sports. He was very patient with others and their shortcomings and that, in the long run, speaks volumes for where he is today."

3 YSU:
The Championship Years

The year prior to Tressel taking over at Youngstown State, the Penguins were 5–6. No one expected anything better the next year with Tressel—except Tressel himself. He didn't want to take over the program unless he felt that he could make it a championship-caliber program. Of course, he knew it wasn't going to happen overnight. It was going to take time for players, coaches, athletic administrators, and the community to buy into the new regime. But Tressel was steadfast on turning Youngstown State into a winning program.

It was ugly through the first half of Tressel's inaugural season. But the way he and his team ended the 1986 season was a harbinger of things to come. Heading into the last game of the season, Youngstown State was 1–9. The final game was against archrival University of Akron, a school just 40 miles away, featuring first-year coach Gerry Faust, a candidate for the Youngstown State job that eventually went to Tressel. The YSU-Akron rivalry now had an added level of intrigue because of the two first-year coaches. Vince Peterson, defensive lineman and a senior that year, witnessed a transformation of the program in that one game.

"The last game of that '86 season was also the last game of my career," said Peterson. "It was against our rival, the University of Akron, and we were 1–9. Coach Tressel brought in a speaker from Ohio State to talk to us the day before the game. I remember being in the locker room after practice and this guy talking about team unity. He and Coach Tressel were standing in the corner. This man kept

After defeating Marshall to win one of four Division I-AA national championships, Tressel and his players take a moment in the locker room to celebrate.

saying, 'You guys have got to get closer, literally.' He actually made us sit closer to one another. We were really pushed together, then he said, 'No, you need a tighter bond. You need to get even closer.' At that moment, it was almost like I could feel my teammates' heartbeats and adrenaline, each and every one of them. It was such a rush. I remember I was in tears. I was honestly in tears and that's the only time I've ever cried in football. It was so tight in that locker room that Coach Tressel was squished in the corner to where he was almost in a sitting position. And that guy from Ohio State said, 'Now this is how close you guys have got to be tomorrow.'"

Akron was 8–2 at that time and needed a win to get into the Division I-AA playoffs. Youngstown State won the game 40–39 in the last second. "That was the start of something great at YSU and I can tell you, to this day, it was because of us coming together as a team during that meeting," Peterson said.

That victory was the first stepping stone of Tressel's career. People complained that the university had fired the previous coach and brought a 33-year-old rookie who had only one win going into the last game against the school's archrival. But coming from behind and beating Akron the way Youngstown State did changed the whole complexion of the program. The recruiting got better and Tressel was able to bring better players in. The program took off from there.

"I remember going to Youngstown State games before Tressel got there and they didn't have 1,000 fans in the stands. The first year for Jim was the same," Geletka said. "But each year, the program got better and better, to where you had a full house at Stambaugh Stadium. The biggest thing you saw with Jim and his programs at Youngstown State and Ohio State is that from the beginning of the season and as you moved on into the season, his teams got better and better. I remember in 1991, watching Youngstown State play Slippery Rock, and it was really a lackluster game. I mean we really could have lost that game. I said to someone after the game, 'We won't win five games.' Well, we turned it around and won the national championship that year."

Former Youngstown State fullback Steve Jones remembers the lean years. He played for the Penguins from 1986 to 1989. He never played for a national championship, but he was part of Tressel's initial wave of players who helped set the foundation for what was to come.

"I had already been at YSU before Coach Tressel got there, so his first year was all about getting adjusted to him and his coaching philosophy and style," Jones said. "My sophomore year, we were 1–9 before we won our last game against Akron. It seemed like it took us to

STEVE JONES

Position: Fullback

Hometown: Youngstown, Ohio

Years Played: 1986–1989

Career Highlights: Jones was a very effective blocking back who also was a hard runner. A consistent receiver out of the backfield, he is tied for ninth on the school's all-time career receptions list with 101.

the second-to-the-last game until we started to turn into a team that could play together."

In 1987, YSU reached the I-AA playoffs before losing to Northern Iowa in the first round, in a game that was decided in the final seconds. But it was another positive step in the right direction for Tressel and the program. The 1989 season was met with some adversity. The Penguins started the season 0–2 and there were concerns about whether or not Tressel would last through the remainder of the season. It was rumored that if Youngstown State didn't win the next game against Akron, Tressel would be fired. "That Akron game, the third week of the season, after we had lost our first two games, and after everyone thought this was going to be our year, was a must-win for us because we all thought Coach Tressel's head was on the chopping block," Jones said. "We had all been there with him for two years and we really liked him."

YSU trailed Akron in a close contest late in the game. The key to the Penguins' drive was converting on two huge fourth-down plays. Then, they were inside Akron's 20 on third-and-long. All that was going through Jones' head was a conversation he had with Tressel at the beginning of the season. "During the first two weeks of the season, I kept joking with Coach Tressel about throwing me the ball more out of the backfield," Jones said. "I told him if he ever started throwing me the ball, he could count on me to go up and go get it." Jones finally got his wish, with the game hanging in the balance. The Penguins were in their huddle on third-and-long and quarterback Ray "the Colonel" Isaac surprisingly called Jones' play. Jones' eyes lit up with excitement and after Isaac finished calling the play, and before the Penguins broke the huddle, Jones said, "It's game time, baby." Jones ran the pattern out of the backfield. The defensive back forced Jones out of bounds momentarily, which allowed him to come back onto the field and still be eligible to make a catch. At that point, Isaac, who was being pressured, had already thrown the pass. The safety and the cornerback were closing in on Jones in the end zone ready to potentially break up the pass. If Youngstown State didn't score on that play, they would more than likely lose the game.

Jones had other thoughts going through his mind at that moment. "I was in the back of the end zone thinking, *If I don't make a play on this ball, the game is over and Coach Tressel is gone.*" He went up for the ball, gave one of the two defensive backs a nudge, just enough to give him a little space to make the catch. "When I came down with the ball, the ref was standing right next to me and I just knew he was going to call pass interference on me. But if I didn't push one of the defensive backs, just a little, the ball was going to be intercepted. I caught the ball to win the game and I remember Akron's coach Gerry Faust, who was the coach at Notre Dame before he was fired, went crazy. When we left the field and walked down the tunnel into the locker rooms, you could still hear him yelling and screaming."

> *"I was in the back of the end zone thinking, If I don't make a play on this ball, the game is over and Coach Tressel is gone."*

Starting with the Akron win, Youngstown State won seven in a row and nine of its next 10 games. "Youngstown State fans will always talk about all the national championships that the program has played in and won, but they also talk about the '89 team as the team that started to build that proud tradition, a program to be reckoned with," Jones said. "We made it to the second round of the playoffs that year."

Jones graduated and the following year the 1990 team went undefeated in the regular season before losing a heartbreaker on a last-second field goal at home to Central Florida in the first round of the playoffs. But in 1991, Ray Isaac, at quarterback, led the team to its first of four national championship titles.

And that first national championship was indeed magical. Just ask Carmen Cassese. If you ask around, people will tell you that Carmen

Tressel always had a watchful eye on everything that was going on with his players on the field.

Cassese was the face of Youngstown State football. Or at least the "face mask" of YSU football. He had been the equipment manager for the Penguins for nearly 30 years. He owned the popular Italian family restaurant MVR, which stands for Mahoning Valley Restaurant, right in the heart of YSU country. The Cassese family and the Tressel family were very close.

During the '91 season, Youngstown State was 4–3 after the first seven games and Week 8 was a must-win game. The challenge was that the game was at perennial power Georgia Southern. The Penguins needed to win the rest of their games to make the playoffs and a loss at Georgia Southern would have ended any playoff hopes. YSU was a huge underdog going into the matchup. It was supposed to be the year that the Eagles were a lock to win the national championship because the title game was going to be played on their home field in Statesboro.

With the odds against them, the Penguins just prepared for what Tressel always talked about: the task at hand. Nothing else mattered except that game, because a loss meant a postseason appearance would be gone. Youngstown State marched into Statesboro and battled Georgia Southern right down to the wire. In the end, the Penguins won 19–17 in what was the turning point of that national championship season. But the interesting story is what took place after the win. As the Youngstown State buses were chugging away from Georgia Southern's stadium, Tressel asked the bus drivers to stop the vehicles right there on the side of the road.

"Georgia Southern had written the standard and we had read everything we could read about them and studied them like crazy," Tressel said. "And one of the things they always talked about was that they always had magic in that Eagle Creek."

That's where Tressel had the buses stop. Cassese was sitting right next to Tressel on the lead bus. "I remember we stopped on the side of the road and me and Coach Tressel went down a ledge or this

33

ravine and we scooped up some water and put it in a jar," Cassese said. "I'll never forget Coach Tressel asking that bus driver to stop the bus on the side of the road. I can still see him going to the river bank with me, and when we got back on the bus, the players were dumbfounded. They didn't know what Coach and I were doing."

Cassese was responsible for getting that jar of "magic water" back to Youngstown. Once the team arrived in Youngstown, Tressel told Cassese to go down to the banks of the Mahoning River, scoop up some water from their hometown river, and mix it in with the magic water from Eagle Creek. "It was funny because I've been in Youngstown my whole life and I see that river every day, but I didn't even know where to go to get water from the Mahoning," Caseese said. "So I had to go get our old equipment manager Chubby Scott to show me where to get the water because Chubby used to swim in the Mahoning River. He showed me a path and we went down there. I got the water and mixed it and brought it back to my office, where it sat."

Tressel, the ultimate motivator, had a plan. No one knew what that plan was except him. That Georgia Southern win started a streak of seven consecutive wins for YSU, which put the Penguins into the national championship game at Georgia Southern, this time against Marshall.

"After we beat Georgia Southern, we said if we earned the right to get a victory and we get to take a little bit of that water home with us, which we did, we would take it home and mix it with a little Mahoning River water and we had in our mind that we were going to go back there to Statesboro," Tressel said. "Our goal was we were going to take that water back there to Statesboro to play in the national championship and we were going to sprinkle the field with a little bit of our own magic water."

"I brought that water along and when we beat Marshall for our first national championship, we poured that water out on the field. It

Tressel always enjoyed watching his players celebrate the spoils of their success and hard work, as they did after winning a national championship in Huntington, West Virginia.

was so symbolic of the focus we had as team that year and that focus helped us become national champs," Cassese said.

Former YSU wide receiver Herb Williams said one of his greatest memories playing for the Penguins was during that '91 season. It was his play in the first round of a home playoff game against Villanova that helped the Penguins come from behind and continue their improbable march to winning a national championship. YSU trailed Villanova 16–14 with less than two minutes left. The

Penguins had the ball at their own 41 on fourth-and-11. The season was on the verge of being over. Williams ran a post pattern and Isaac threw the ball in Williams' vicinity, but the ball was tipped by a defender. That's when everything went into slow motion for Williams.

"In my head, I was like, *Oh noooooo!* But then I knew that I couldn't blow it. I went up for it and caught it with one hand as I was coming down to the ground for a 41-yard reception. When I came down, it seemed like everything was silent. I didn't realize how big of a catch it was until I got up and saw everyone cheering."

The play helped set up a 33-yard game-winning field goal by Jeff Wilkins (who would play in the NFL for 14 years, including two Super Bowls with the St. Louis Rams) with no time remaining for a 17–16 win. "That's when I truly realized what it took to be a winner," Williams said. "And I really believe to this day that that catch helped define me as a man. Being able to focus, concentrate, have faith in myself and my teammates, but, more than anything else, to never give up on yourself."

"Herb caught that big pass for us and I know he thinks it was a catch that defined him as a man but I don't know if I would say that the catch defined him as a man," Tressel said. "It defined him in the outside world but not for us. We saw the road he had taken to get to that point. If you wanted the chance for someone to come down with the ball, we all learned that it didn't matter how fast you ran or anything like that, if you wanted the ball caught, throw it to Herbie. Then the world saw that with that catch he made and he made plenty more down the road."

Tressel said when Williams was in high school, the athlete thought he was going to the NBA. He didn't start playing football until his junior year, but he was such an outstanding athlete that he helped take his team at Boardman (Ohio) High School to the state championship. Williams was the standout on that team, but no one showed up to recruit him other than Youngstown State. Williams didn't get a scholarship from Tressel, just money for books, and it wasn't much.

"For a guy where things hadn't gone the way he dreamed, he didn't let that affect him," Tressel said about Williams. "He humbled himself and just said, 'OK I'm going to go to work.' We actually put Herb on defense at first and he was a cornerback. Then we moved him over to offense as a wide receiver. It took him a little while to get into the lineup, but yet he caught everything in practice. He couldn't run quite as well as some of the other guys, but he was better than they were. But he didn't let that bother him. He stayed humble, he didn't bellyache, he didn't complain—he just continued to show what he could do. He was just humble enough to fight through the shattered dreams and the long road he had to take to become the go-to wide receiver for us, then he became the man for us."

The 1991 season was the first of four consecutive national championship appearances Youngstown State made, winning three ('91, '93, '94). The 1992 national championship was a heartbreaker for the Penguins; they lost 31–28 to Marshall at their home field in Huntington, West Virginia, on a last-second field goal by Willy Merrick. As Youngstown State's buses headed out of the stadium, Marshall's fans had lined the streets to celebrate, especially outside of the local bars. While the dejected players and coaches on Youngstown buses sat quietly, they could hear the cacophony of fans honking their horns in celebration.

When preseason camp opened for the 1993 season, Tressel, the ultimate motivator, had T-shirts made with "H.O.H, Horns of Huntington" emblazoned on them. The '93 national championship game was in Huntington, and YSU made it back there to play for the national championship, again against Marshall. The Penguins got a chance at redemption and dominated the Thundering Herd, winning 17–5. And on YSU's championship rings, Tressel had the inscription on the side read "H.O.H."

Youngstown State won the national championship again in '94, in a 28–14 victory against Boise State. The next national championship was during the 1997 season, when Youngstown State defeated McNeese State 10–9 on a late touchdown. "When I first got to YSU in 1997, we ran a lot during our preseason conditioning and even during the regular season," said former Penguins wide receiver Damion Matthews, who was a transfer from Indiana University. "I don't think anybody in the country ran as many sprints and worked out as hard as we did. I think that was a big reason why we made it to the national championship that year and beat McNeese State in a defensive battle and a game that went down to the wire. We only had 200 total yards for the game and we were down 9–3 going into the fourth quarter, but pulled out the win."

Surprisingly, Matthews said the following year seemed like a reward atmosphere for the Penguins, which hurt the team. "I don't think we ran as much in 1998 like we did our national championship year in 1997," Williams said. "In 1998, we went 6–5 and didn't make the playoffs."

So, prior to the 1999 season, Tressel brought in every senior and asked them, as a group, "What do we need to do to get better and to get to Chattanooga?" Chattanooga was the site of the national championship game that year. The Penguins had 24 seniors in that meeting. Out of the 24 seniors, 22 of them told Tressel that they needed to run more. "We told him that he didn't make us run as much as we did in '97, when we won the national championship," Matthews said. "I think Coach Tressel took it easy on us the year after we won the national championship in '97. It wasn't like we disrespected Coach Tressel—that wasn't even the case at all. But when he asked us what he thought it would take for us to get back to the national championship, we all felt we needed to work harder. How many athletes do you think would go to a coach and tell him to run you more? But that's what we wanted.

And the great thing about Coach Tressel was that he listened to his players."

Matthews said the workouts during the '99 season were brutal, but the players didn't care because they eventually made it to the national championship game in Chattanooga against Georgia Southern. The Penguins lost 59–24, but Matthews said the team was proud of the way they rebounded after the 1998 season, making it all the way to the national championship game. "The way Coach Tressel brought us together as a team and what he did for our senior class that year was something that helped build me into who I am today, no question," said Matthews, who caught the winning touchdown in the semifinal win against Florida A & M late in the game to help Youngstown State reach the national championship. "He got us to believe in each other and trust one another."

Matthews was a Florida transplant who initially started his career at the University of Indiana. When Matthews was recruited by YSU, he didn't know anything about Youngstown, or Ohio for that matter. Mark Snyder, who coached with Tressel at YSU and Ohio State and is now the head coach at Marshall, recruited Matthews at YSU. "When I first arrived at YSU, we were at a team meeting and this guy was talking," Matthews said. "About 45 seconds after listening to this guy talk, I said to myself, *This man needs to run for President.* My friend from Florida, Antonio Page, was sitting next to me. I tapped him on the shoulder and said, 'Who is that guy?' Antonio responded, 'That's the head coach. That's Jim Tressel.' So within 45 seconds of just seeing and listening to this guy for the very first time, I felt like he should be the President of the United States. That was the effect he had on me in just the first 45 seconds that I ever met Coach Tressel. He is just a great person to be around and listen to. The things that come out of his mouth are so motivating that you have no choice but to be a winner if you stay around him for a certain period of time."

Cassese, meanwhile, said that during Youngstown State's successful run in the '90s, the program was highly respected across the country. When the Penguins played on the road, they played in front of packed stadiums. "You could tell that teams and fans were in awe of us," Cassese said proudly. "Everybody wanted to be us. It's kind of funny, when we started winning national championships, all of a sudden I became a smarter equipment man.... I'd be getting calls from all over the country from equipment people who would ask me, 'What shoulder pads are you using? What spikes are you using?' Here, I'm the same person I was years ago, but because we're winning, now all of a sudden I'm the smartest guy in the world because I'm buying the right pads and the right helmets. Everyone now wanted advice from me. I was on committees with Division I guys who wanted my advice. It was a great feeling when we were bused into a stadium the day before and some of us would be wearing our national championship rings. That was the sign of excellence. We were able to walk the walk. It was an amazing time."

But that magical time for Youngstown State fans came to an end when Tressel accepted the job at Ohio State. Prior to that, in the 15 years Tressel was at Youngstown State, he had built a unique friendship with Cassese and their respective families. Tressel's son, Zach, loved woodworking and so did Cassese, so they would often work on projects together. Cassese's restaurant also helped bring the two families together. "Coach Tressel was very loyal to me," Cassese said. "He came here with his whole family after every game. There may have been a game or two he missed for whatever reason, but by and large, his whole family had their own table here after every game and that meant a lot to me. He was always an MVR guy, and when you have a place that's been in your family for 80 years, it's a personal thing. It's like having someone at your house."

Tressel's departure from Youngstown State for Ohio State wasn't a predetermined goal for him, as some may have thought.

Youngstown was never intended to be a pit stop on Tressel's fast-track to a Division I head coaching position. "I never really had a timeline saying I wanted to be in I-A by this time," Tressel said. "My belief always was something I learned from an athletic director years ago. He said, 'Keep your mind and your rear end in the same place.' He didn't say it exactly that way. He said, 'Then you will be fine.' And I heeded that advice because wherever I was, I was always working only on that, and then when the proper times came when you could have some considerations about other things, assess the opportunities, made decisions, and then went back to work."

But Ohio State wasn't seeking out Tressel, either. "Ohio State didn't really come to me. I called Ohio State in this particular case," Tressel said. "When it came along at the time it came along, I threw my hat in the ring and kind of talked about 'Here is what I believe and here is how I would proceed.' Thank goodness [former Ohio State athletic director] Andy Geiger and his committee decided to give me a chance. And is it a dream job? I grew up in Ohio. I coached in Ohio. Of course it would be more of a dream than some other place miles and miles away. But I didn't wake up every morning dreaming about going there. I woke up every morning working at Youngstown State."

Cassese said that when Tressel got the Ohio State job, Tressel wanted to make the transition from Youngstown to Columbus with as little fanfare as possible. "He asked me to pack everything up and it was like a bittersweet moment," Cassese said. "Obviously I wanted him to go to Ohio State, but I hated to lose him. It was an incredible moment, just sitting in his office and looking at everything that was in there and knowing that the era was over. It was something special. It was a very emotional and historic moment for me."

Naturally, Tressel's time at Youngstown State was emotional and historic as well. "You know, those years in Youngstown really helped me understand how much impact a good football program could have," Tressel said. "I always appreciated football and had grown up with it and thought it was important. But all of a sudden, when you are in Youngstown and you see the way a group of people rallies around a group of kids and rallies around some success and perhaps at a time they needed it, that really etched in stone my understanding of how important it can be to people bigger than yourself. Bigger than you winning the game or making your goals."

They were goals that he would take with him to Columbus, and to the Buckeyes of The Ohio State University.

4 The Quarterback's Quarterback

Jim Tressel was a quarterback from his youth through his college days. His athletic ability and academic achievement formed a perfect pedigree for him to be a team leader. And so he was at Berea High School and at Baldwin-Wallace College, where he played for his father.

It was only natural that, as a coach, he would hone in on quarterbacks. Coming up the ranks, he made a name for himself as a well-respected and highly regarded quarterbacks coach. And over the years as a head coach, Tressel developed unique relationships with his quarterbacks.

Former Youngstown State quarterback Mark Brungard, who went on to become the head coach at Poland (Ohio) Seminary High School, was on four national championship teams and played in three. He is probably the most successful quarterback to ever play for Tressel, a fact that Brungard would be embarrassed to even discuss.

Tressel had seen Brungard play, and knew he wanted the quarterback to play for him at YSU. He employed an ingenious recruiting tactic to get him there.

"I lived on a farm, and our family sold Christmas trees during the holidays," Brungard said. "My senior year in high school was 1990, and that year YSU went 11–0 during the regular season but lost in the first round of the playoffs 20–17, on a last-second field goal.... So they were done early, and...Coach Tressel couldn't go out and start recruiting yet. So during that time, every person on the staff came out and bought a Christmas tree off our farm. That was a little recruiting ploy that he employed, and it worked."

Tressel's unique relationship with his quarterbacks started back during his Youngstown State days.

Brungard was a three-time national champion and played backup on the '92 team that lost to Marshall. He was the winning quarterback in 1994 when the Penguins played Boise State for the I-AA national championship. YSU won, 28–14.

"Every person on the staff came out and bought a Christmas tree off our farm. That was a little recruiting ploy that he employed, and it worked."

Brungard saw the Boise State program go from one that YSU handled fairly easily to a program that shot to national Division I prominence in 2007, when the Broncos played in one of college football's greatest games (another instant classic) in the Fiesta Bowl. Boise State shocked Oklahoma and the world by beating the Sooners 43–42 in overtime.

The same season that Youngstown State won the national championship against Boise State, they had to beat a talented Alcorn State team that featured Heisman Trophy candidate Steve McNair in a first-round matchup that carried a lot of hype with it. McNair and Alcorn State were lighting up teams and putting up points that sounded more like basketball scores. It was not unusual for Alcorn State to line up with five wide receivers, then let McNair pick apart a secondary. He did it all season in his senior year.

Against Youngstown State, McNair set a Division I-AA playoff record for attempts (82) and completions (52) and his 514 passing yards were three short of a record. But Alcorn State still lost 63–20.

Brungard said Tressel's best coaching that week was in keeping the team relaxed and focused. There was more hype surrounding the game than any Youngstown State had ever played. ESPN moved the game to the Friday after Thanksgiving so that it could be the featured game.

"That was the most jacked up our team had ever been for a game, and our defense had the most pressure on them," Brungard said.

"You couldn't really stop McNair. All you could do was hope to contain him."

Youngstown State caught a break. McNair suffered a leg injury prior to the game and wasn't 100 percent healthy. He was operating with limited mobility—and that was a huge component of his potent arsenal. He could beat you with his strong arm and pinpoint accuracy, but he could hurt you even more with his running ability.

It was all the advantage the defense needed. They even scored—twice. One was a 93-yard interception return by All-American linebacker Leon Jones, and the other a fumble recovery for a touchdown by All-American defensive back Randy Smith.

Brungard said that game is still one of his most memorable moments at YSU. "The first time McNair threw the ball, we sacked him, he fumbled it, and we picked it up and recovered it," Brungard said. "It was so loud, and that was even before we had the other side to the stadium." For years, Stambaugh Stadium had just one side of seats for spectators. And against Alcorn State, like most home games under Tressel, the stands were filled to near capacity.

As much success as Brungard had in his five years with the YSU program, he feels that it was the losing that made him a better person, a better coach, and a better educator. In his final year, the Penguins finished a dismal 3–8.

"That was obviously one of the most frustrating times in my sports career and in my life, but at the same time it was one of [growth]," Brungard said. "Coach Tressel came into the locker room after that last game and his eyes welled up with tears."

Outside the locker room, there was a group of children gathered. They were excited to get the opportunity to slap a player on the shoulder pads, or, even better, get a chance to actually high-five a player. It didn't matter to them that YSU had just lost its eighth game of the season. Those players were their heroes.

"Coach Tressel made a point, with tears in his eyes, that we needed to always remember that it's not always about winning the game," Brungard said. "It was about those kids, and who you were to those kids. Coach Tressel shifted the focus right there and then to what it was really about. He was about building men who were not about building successful lives for themselves, but building men to serve others, to give back to their communities and be impact people in their communities."

5 Eloise Tressel Remembered

Inside Jim and Ellen Tressel's luxury box at Ohio Stadium is a picture of his mother, Eloise, who died of pancreatic and liver cancer at the age of 76, just a few weeks shy of her son's Ohio State debut. The picture hangs on a wall with an inscription that embodies Eloise Tressel's dynamic spirit:

> First and 10, let's do it again!
> —Eloise Tressel

"Eloise was such a cheerleader for Berea High School, where Jim was the star quarterback," said longtime family friend Jackie Groza, widow of Hall of Fame Browns kicker Lou "the Toe" Groza. The Groza and Tressel families lived in Berea, a suburb of Cleveland. Mrs. Groza saw the development of Tressel from an accomplished student-athlete to an accomplished coach.

"Jim looked up to his dad so much and I think he also looked up to my husband," Mrs. Groza said. "As a kid, Jim was always at the field at Baldwin-Wallace when Lou would go over there to practice kicking. Lou would start in June every summer, and Jim, our sons, and so many kids would go over and shag balls for Lou. That was so much fun for the kids. They looked up to Lou because he was this professional football player, but Lou loved all the kids, and they loved him.

"It's just so sad she never got a chance to watch Jim coach a game at Ohio State."

Tressel was the starting quarterback for Sandy Madzy's husband, the late Tom Madzy, at Berea and Sandy was like another mother to Tressel. The three wives—Madzy, Tressel, and Groza—were friends for many, many years. They grew close because of their association with the game of football.

"One of my first introductions to Eloise was when my husband got the job at Berea," Madzy said. "She always came to the games. One time, I turned around to someone and said, 'Who is that lady screaming back there?' The person said, 'Oh, you haven't met Eloise Tressel yet?' She was a bundle of enthusiasm and we loved her. We love the entire Tressel family."

Jim Tressel remembers those times. "There's nothing like a mother's love. And when you start talking about my mom and Jackie Groza and Sandy Madzy, those were three moms in my life as I was growing up," Tressel said. "And there's nothing like your high school coach. You'll do anything to please your high school coach, and I had the opportunity to get to know Mrs. Madzy while I was playing for her husband. And of course, I went to [Baldwin-Wallace College] right there in the same community, so to keep the relationships over those years was special.

"No matter how you're doing in your career, if you have those mother figures, they always give you that little look like, *You'll be fine. You'll be OK. You'll succeed,*" Tressel said. "So it was awfully special to me to be able to bring them to Columbus for the interview when I got the job because it was because of their encouragement, their love, their total confidence in me that made me feel special— and that's what mothers are all about."

Mrs. Madzy loved telling the story about the time that Coach Tressel stayed with her family for a few days. He was a "perfect young man," she recalls, "and he always made sure he drank his milk.

"Eloise and Lee had gone down to their home in Florida for a brief period of time and my husband invited Jim to come to dinner," Mrs. Madzy said. "Jim was playing quarterback for my husband—I think he was a junior at the time—and our son, Tom, was a lot younger than Jim. Tom was maybe in the fifth or sixth grade, and he just sat at the dinner table and he couldn't eat. He just watched Jim the whole night. Jim had milk to drink with his dinner and our son never drank milk with his dinner. He did that night. He wanted to do everything Jim did. I thought, *If Jim has such a big impact on Tom like that, he ought to come to dinner more often.*"

The three ladies were extremely excited about their road trip to Columbus, when the school held a press conference to announce Tressel was the new Buckeyes coach. They felt like young college coeds on a road trip.

"Eloise called me the day before to say that they were going to make the announcement that Jimmy—or should I say Jim—would be the football coach at Ohio State, and that she was inviting Mrs. Madzy and myself to go down to Columbus with her," Mrs. Groza said. "We were all so excited and happy for Jim and Eloise because they're such a nice family. So we left early in the morning and we were there for the news conference."

Shortly after arriving in Columbus, the ladies pulled up to park when they heard someone shouting, "Eloise Tressel! Eloise Tressel!" It was former YSU quarterback Jared Zwick, older brother of former Ohio State quarterback Justin Zwick, who was attending Ohio State's dental school. It was just another reminder of the influence that the Tressel family had on Jim's football "family."

It was a special day for Tressel, his mother, and her dear friends. "The day they had the press conference at Ohio State to announce Jim as the new head coach, he pulled me aside at one point and said, 'I wish would've been able to have my Mom *and* Dad here,'" Geletka recalled. "Jim did say that he felt his Dad is with him all the time. And as we went down to the press conference, he said to me, 'Just make sure that my mother, Mrs. Groza, Mrs. Madzy, and the other ladies get seats. It's very important to me so watch for them at the door.'"

And the ladies felt like stars as well. Like the press conference was also in their honor, in a sense. "We were introduced and went up to where the press conference was, and Eloise just glowed. She handled the press like a pro," Mrs. Madzy said. "That's the kind of lady she was, so outgoing and such a warm person."

After the press conference, Jim had to go over to the basketball arena to make a speech to the OSU faithful. The speech that Tressel made at Ohio State's Value City Arena during halftime of a OSU-Michigan basketball game was historic. "I can assure you that you will be proud of your young people in the classroom, in the community, and most especially in 310 days in Ann Arbor, Michigan, on the football field," Tressel told the cheering crowd.

> *"You have a lot of help coaching, Jim. Your dad and your mom and my husband are all up in heaven pulling for you."*

Meanwhile, the ladies were enjoying dinner together. "We had such a good time," Mrs. Groza said. "Shortly after that, Eloise became very ill. She was not living when Jim coached his very first game at Ohio State and I still can't get over that.... We all loved her so much. Everyone did."

Madzy remembers the day Mrs. Tressel passed away. "Her calling hours were at Ursprung, which is Baldwin-Wallace's gymnasium complex. Her Memorial Service was in Finney Stadium, and it was packed. For the people who stood in the long lines outside the gym waiting to get in and see the family, it was very befitting for a great lady to have a beautiful day like that. She would have loved all of her friends coming together and telling [their] Eloise stories.

"We felt kind of cheated for Eloise when she passed away. Jim got the Ohio State job in January or February of 2001...and Eloise passed away in August. She was such a cheerleader for Jim and such a proud, good mom. And she would have loved to go down to Columbus, sit in that box, and do her cheerleading from there. If she were alive to see Jim take the field for the first time at Ohio State, get his first win, and win the national championship like he did, she would have simply said, 'That's my boy. I've always known you could do it.'

"After Jim got the job at Ohio State, I told him, 'You have a lot of help coaching, Jim. Your dad and your mom and my husband are all up in heaven pulling for you.' He just looked at me and proudly smiled."

In 2008, Tressel lost a close and personal friend with ties to his family. Bob Packard, who coached Tressel at Baldwin-Wallace and was the winningest football coach in the school's history, died of a heart attack at age 64. Packard was an assistant coach under Tressel's father, Lee, who is in the College Football Hall of Fame. Packard succeeded Lee Tressel in 1981 and coached 20 seasons.

Tressel remembers Packard as another influential person who helped shape him as a player, a coach, a man. "The experience I had growing up at Baldwin-Wallace and watching football every day—our house was next door to the stadium. I got to watch my dad do what he loved and [watch] my position. Coach Bob Packard ending up being the head coach for 20 years after my dad's passing, and being around guys like that who were so successful, just accidentally maybe you pick up some good things if you are paying attention at all.

"Here at Ohio State, we wake up every day hopefully counting our blessings. You reflect a little bit about the sum total of your experiences, and [are] blessed to be where you are from a career standpoint. A lot of it began right there with my dad and Coach Packard, and it happened to be Baldwin-Wallace College."

6 A Man of Class

When Tressel got the job at Ohio State, he was excited about the future. But at the same time, he realized he needed to go back in the past. One of the first things he did was contact former Buckeyes head coaches John Cooper and Earle Bruce. Tressel wanted these two men to be associated with the program once again.

Cooper was the head coach from 1988 to 2000 and compiled a 111–43–4 record with the Buckeyes. During his tenure, he produced quality NFL players including 1995 Heisman Trophy winner Eddie George, the late Korey Stringer, 1996 Outland Trophy winner Orlando Pace, Robert Smith, Joey Galloway, Terry Glenn, Mike Vrabel, and Antoine Winfield. But the Ohio State faithful know that his 2–10–1 record against Michigan was a major reason why he was dismissed.

Bruce coached the Buckeyes from 1979–1987, taking over the job after legendary coach Woody Hayes was fired. Bruce compiled an 81–26–1 record in nine seasons with the Buckeyes and was inducted into the College Football Hall of Fame in 2002.

"Feeling like you're part of the family is very important," Cooper said. "When you talk about Ohio State, there's a saying, 'Once a Buckeye, always a Buckeye.' It's about the importance of loyalty and family, and that's where I give Jim a lot of credit. The one sad thing about Ohio State is that you can't find very many coaches who have left happy. It's a fact. If you go back, I'll ask you to name me one coach—not only in football—name me one coach who's ever left Ohio State happy. Not Woody Hayes, not Earle Bruce, not John

Cooper, and not [basketball coaches] Jim O'Brien or Randy Ayers. You might say [basketball coach] Gary Williams left happy because he went to Maryland and had a nice deal there, but I guess what I'm saying is in the past, they don't treat you very good when you leave Ohio State.

"But Jim is the first coach that I know of at Ohio State to have an office there at the Woody Hayes Complex for Earle and [me]," Cooper said. "What does that mean? It means we'll hang out over there more. And we feel a little more welcome. We're all in the business of trying to help Ohio State win football games. If Earle Bruce or John Cooper can help to recruit and influence a player in any way to come to Ohio State, then that's a positive thing. And we're not threats to anybody's jobs. Earle's not going to coach anymore; I'm not going to coach anymore. We're beyond that, so all we're trying to do now is help the university in any way we possibly can. And any way Jim can use that to his advantage, we call that the winners edge." Others call it a classy gesture on Tressel's part. But it is what Tressel is all about.

And for the record, Cooper said he never had any animosity toward Tressel when he was brought on to replace him. "Obviously, any successful coach has a big ego," Cooper said. "You have pride, and you're hurt when you're let go. Was I happy about that move? Absolutely not. But Jim didn't have anything to do with getting me out of my job here at Ohio State. It was one guy and that was [former Ohio State athletic director] Andy Geiger. And now that Geiger's gone, I feel a lot more comfortable about being around the program. I didn't have any animosity toward Jim. Heck, they had to hire somebody."

Tressel always had respect for his colleagues, even when they were his rivals, like former longtime Michigan coach Lloyd Carr. When Carr left Michigan with a 41–35 win against Florida in the 2008 Capital One Bowl, it was a feather in his cap. Carr, a well-respected man in the collegiate ranks for decades, went out on top.

It was probably the only time in his life that Tressel was happy to see Michigan win. "I felt great," Tressel said about Carr winning the last game of his career in the bowl game. "Lloyd Carr is one of the great gentlemen in our profession. To see his team respond and play so well, and obviously they're members of our conference, we're proud of that. And Lloyd Carr has had an extraordinary career. If you look at his resume of what he's accomplished, it's always nice for someone to end that way."

Former Ohio State wide receiver Anthony Gonzalez said what he learned most during his career at Ohio State from 2003 to 2006 and playing for Tressel was that class always mattered—and it could never be compromised, in victory or defeat.

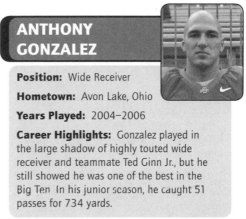

ANTHONY GONZALEZ

Position: Wide Receiver

Hometown: Avon Lake, Ohio

Years Played: 2004–2006

Career Highlights: Gonzalez played in the large shadow of highly touted wide receiver and teammate Ted Ginn Jr., but he still showed he was one of the best in the Big Ten In his junior season, he caught 51 passes for 734 yards.

Gonzalez burst onto the scene at Ohio State as a junior in 2005 and one of his more memorable plays was his acrobatic 26-yard catch at Michigan that set up the game-winning touchdown two plays later with 37 seconds left, giving the Buckeyes a 25–21 win. The following year, Gonzalez proved to be one of the top clutch receivers in the country. He eventually was a first-round draft pick by the Indianapolis Colts in the 2007 NFL draft.

What was more important to Gonzalez was going into the NFL with a classy organization like the Indianapolis Colts, who had a classy coach in Tony Dungy. "It's very easy today to be turned off by people without class," Gonzalez said. "And you don't necessarily recognize those that are very classy unless it's something that is so profound about their character. You certainly recognize individuals who lack class. It's always been important to me to represent myself with class and dignity and major character. That's really where the class aspect came into my approach toward football.

"The team, organization, and any group effort is usually a reflection of its leader or leaders, and Coach Tressel has always shown great class and has always been a classy individual for as long as I've known him and as long as the state of Ohio and the country [have] known him. I think that naturally filters itself down to the players and everyone involved with the program to the point where it is now, which is a program that is well-respected and thought of very highly throughout the country."

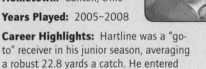

BRIAN HARTLINE

Position: Wide Receiver
Hometown: Canton, Ohio
Years Played: 2005–2008
Career Highlights: Hartline was a "go-to" receiver in his junior season, averaging a robust 22.8 yards a catch. He entered the NFL draft after his junior season, but continued on to earn his degree in 2009.

When the Buckeyes lost the 2006 national championship to Florida in a game that the Gators dominated, many Ohio State players said it could have been easy to not show class. At least that's how Buckeyes wide receiver Brian Hartline felt. Ohio State was favored in that game, but many critics felt the Buckeyes were too full of themselves and read too many of their own press clippings. When Ohio State was overpowered by Florida, the Buckeyes offered no excuses.

"I think the biggest thing I took away from Coach Tressel's postgame team speech after we lost the national championship against Florida was something he has always preached, and it was always show class," said Hartline, whose first year at Ohio State was 2005. Hartline, who was one of the top hurdlers in the state his senior year at Canton (Ohio) GlenOak High School. He redshirted his freshman season but he showed his talent in 2006.

"It was the idea that we represented a nation," Hartline said. "We represent the Buckeye Nation, and when we lost, Coach Tressel looked at us and said, 'You know you guys worked hard. I can't take that away from you guys. You did some things but it didn't happen.' He talked about how the guys who were coming back next year, it was our turn to take the torch, and that it's always a process, it's always a journey, and it never ends. The season may have ended, but the journey was not done. He always preached that no matter what we did and whatever the outcome, we needed to show class. And I think we did that against Florida. Sure, it hurt to lose, but we showed class in defeat."

Legendary Ohio State running back Archie Griffin (1972–1975), a two-time Heisman Trophy winner, said, "The one thing that came out of the Florida loss was that Ohio State showed that class still mattered. Our players gave Florida credit. Our players said Florida was a better team than we were. It was one of those situations where, as John Cooper would say, 'the dog didn't hunt.' They didn't make any excuses."

And showing class was Tressel's calling card, all the way back to his days at YSU. At the time he was hired at YSU, the city and the area were going through some tough times. "We had lost the steel mills, we had a little bit of a reputation as being a rough town and there wasn't anything glamorous at that point about Youngstown State," Tressel said. "But what we always talked about was with all that not-withstanding, we still have our class and they can't take away. How we play, how we carry ourselves is most important. Ultimately, we'll get better and better and better and our class will give us a chance to stand at the top of the mountain. In fact, we used to always say, 'There are a lot of great teams that may be good enough to be champions, but it's the team with class that's going to ultimately stand at the top of the mountain.'"

Former YSU running back Archie Herring was one of those players who helped lay the foundation for the Penguins' ultimate success in the 1990s, although Herring never played in a national championship game. His timing may have been off in that department, but the four years he spent playing under Tressel and learning from him were just as gratifying as winning a national championship.

Herring was a unique Tressel recruit. He wasn't known for his size (he was about 5'7", and that was a stretch) but he was one of the strongest and fastest running backs the Penguins ever had. He led YSU in rushing in 1989 (with 1,095 yards and 12 touchdowns) and in 1990 (with 904 yards and 11 touchdowns). In 1990, he helped lead YSU to an undefeated 11–0 regular season. Unfortunately, the Penguins lost 20–17 at home to Central Florida on a last-second field goal in the first round of the Division I-AA playoffs.

Herring said that class was one of the things Tressel talked about every single day. Herring told a story about one of his teammates, quarterback Ray Isaac, making the second start of his career in a game against Eastern Michigan University. "Ray threw some crazy pass that was intercepted," Herring recalled. "Then, all of a sudden, Coach Tressel was on the sideline screaming, 'Ray. Why did you throw that pass? That was dumb.' Then Coach Tressel kind of shut down and pulled back. That was the only time I've ever heard Coach Tressel yell."

Herring said when the team got back to Youngstown the next day and was together for a meeting, he saw first hand what Tressel meant by always having class. Herring said the first thing Tressel did at the meeting was address his actions. "In front of the whole team and coaching staff, Coach Tressel said, 'The first thing I want to do is apologize to Ray for saying some words to him that I shouldn't have said. I should have never done that. It was very unprofessional. I shouldn't have said that and I should have respected you more and you'll never hear that out of me again.' After seeing that class act, I had so much reverence for Coach Tressel. He's not going to berate you and he's not going to make you feel like less of a man."

He told another story about not being classy, which dealt specifically with him. The Penguins were playing at Bowling Green. It was halftime and Herring was not having a very good game. Frustrated coming off the field, Herring kicked one of the orange pylons in the corner of the end zone and sent it flying about 10 yards. What Herring didn't know was that Tressel was just a few feet behind him and saw Herring's classless act. Tressel walked over to the pylon, picked it up and walked back over and put it where it belonged and continued into the locker room.

Tressel didn't say a word to Herring about the incident. When the team came back onto the field for the second half and when Youngstown State's offense went on the field, Herring, who was a starter, remained on the sideline.

"I didn't see a down the rest of the game. That was it for me," Herring said. "Coach Tressel didn't yell at me. He didn't scream at me. I didn't play in the second half and I knew what I did…. I wasn't upset or mad or anything. I learned a valuable lesson about class that Coach Tressel was always trying to teach us. Someone is always watching you and your actions."

Players said Tressel reminded players that on their jerseys, there were two identifiers: the name of the school and the players' last name. He reminded his players that it wasn't about them as individuals; they represented the school and they represented their families.

> "Whether we won or lost, we were going to do it with class, and they set that tone. And everybody who came in after them knew this is the way we do it."

"The first way we better understand what class is all about is the fact that everything we do we're representing our families, each other, the university, and it really wasn't until we knew that it was something bigger than ourselves that we became really good. It started with those guys like Archie Herring and Mike Peterson. They set the standard for the way that we were going to be and we were going to be a team with class," Tressel said.

"Whether we won or lost, we were going to do it with class, and they set that tone. And everybody who came in after them knew this is the way we do it. That was a foundational building block that, without it, we couldn't have reached some of the heights we reached. We used to say, before you can do, you have to be. We just felt like we had to be class before we could do championships. It was in that order. You can't do championships first and then be classy people."

Former YSU linebacker Michael Peterson said he learned a valuable lesson about class during one particular practice. The team was participating in a drill between the offense and defense called "hoot and holler." The drill was so intense that it wasn't unusual for the players from both sides to get into a scuffle, and even the coaches.

The drill consisted of a few offensive linemen and a running back trying to score a touchdown from five yards out on just three plays and in a confined area against the same amount of defensive players. Peterson was one of the defensive players.

"Coach [Ken] Conatser was our offensive coordinator at the time and he said that the offense had scored on a play when they didn't," Peterson said. "I was hot. As a matter of fact, I was so hot—and I don't swear, but things were coming out of my mouth that no one had ever heard. Coach Tressel walked behind me, grabbed me and gently pulled me aside. I don't think anyone else even noticed. Then, he said to me, 'Michael, I understand your intensity, but I don't think your mother and father would be proud of how you just carried yourself.' Coach Tressel is a Christian and his whole thing is—and he told me this later—that you represent God, even in situations like that. He reminded me that not only was God watching and listening, but other people as well."

7 Caring Means More Than Winning

As much as the game of football is a showcase of marvelous speed and tremendous skill, it's easy to forget that it is also a brutal and violent full-contact sport. You hear it from players on the sidelines and on the field all the time—they want to kill their opponents, tear them limb from limb. The sport can lead to serious injury, as it did for former New England Patriots wide receiver Darryl Stingley, who broke his neck getting hit in an exhibition game August 12, 1978. The injury left Stingley a quadriplegic for life. It can even kill. Former NFL player Lyle Alzado, who died of a brain tumor in 1992 at the age 43, said the tumor was a result of his prolonged use of steroids. The game of football is certainly a display of exceptional skill and talent, but it's also a sport of rage.

Yet, even with all the brutality associated with the sport, stripping away all the bravado and machismo, there's an underlying atmosphere of caring and love among these modern-day gladiators that most do not see. Tressel wants to underscore these values to his players.

"I hope my personality is caring," Tressel said. "And I think...one of the things that [young people] want is to be a part of a caring situation. I hope I am demanding because I think players want to be part of a demanding situation when they are as highly passionate about their craft as they are in college football.... I would hope those two are a part of who we are."

Tressel's longtime friend, Bob Mansfield, was one of the men who showed what caring and giving meant. In the mid-'90s, he experienced one of the toughest fights of his life. The healthy former educator and high school athletic official learned he had health problems that required a kidney transplant, and without it he might die. He was devastated. But he was a fighter, he was from Youngstown, and he was intent on fighting to his last breath.

After undergoing a successful kidney transplant, Mansfield vowed to take advantage of every moment he had. A former athlete and someone who remained healthy throughout his adult life, he got himself back in shape by playing a sport he always loved, racquetball. He was so good that he participated in the Transplant Olympics, a national event, in 1998. He actually won the gold medal that year, and then won it again four years later. The medals were prized possessions for Mansfield because they symbolized his triumph over illness.

He remembers receiving a call from Tressel with the news that he had just gotten the Ohio State job. He was thrilled. "I talked to my wife and asked her what I should give Jim for his recent good fortune, and also something as a token of our friendship," Mansfield said. "I wanted to give him something special. If I bought him a box of cigars, they could go bad. He didn't need money, he's making more money than he ever had. Then it hit me. I was going to give him my gold medals that I had won in the Transplant Olympics. They were in a frame hanging in our home, but I wanted to give those to Jim."

The night Tressel drove from Columbus to his home in Youngstown, Mansfield and his wife, Linda, and the Tressels met at the Tressels' home. Tressel had arrived in the dark of night in an attempt to avoid any media attention. Mansfield pulled out the gift and handed it to Tressel. Inside were the medals that Mansfield had won at the Transplant Olympics. All four adults—Mansfield, Tressel, and their two wives—broke down and cried.

"Those medals were the personal things that I cherished the most. But I didn't care because that's how much I valued our friendship,"

Mansfield said. "And the great thing about it is, those medals hang in his office to this day."

And those medals became two of Tressel's most prized possessions. "That was Bob's way of expressing his appreciation for the time when he was struggling and I had the good fortune to be there for him," Tressel said. "He could say 'thank you' and say 'thank you' again and again, but I knew what those medals meant to him and I knew how hard he trained, and for him to want that to be in my possession was a caring and loving gesture on his part. The first thing I did was put it up in my first office when I got here at Ohio State. We've been renovating since then, but it's still right up next to a picture of my dad and me. It holds a special place."

Tressel had a prized possession of his own that he wanted to give to an individual that he cared about, former San Francisco 49ers and Pittsburgh Penguins owner Edward J. DeBartolo Jr. A Youngstown native, DeBartolo, who was once listed 242nd on the *Forbes* list of wealthiest Americans at $5 billion, earned his fortune in real estate development and the shopping mall business. He and Tressel formed a solid friendship during Tressel's 15 years at Youngstown State.

"Jim gave me his ring after YSU won its first national championship game and I cherish it," said DeBartolo, who is also founder of DeBartolo Sports and Entertainment LLC. His agency represents, among other athletes, former Ohio State quarterback and 2006 Heisman Trophy winner Troy Smith. "I'm not a jewelry guy and I don't even wear my Super Bowl rings. But I have that YSU national championship ring on display along with my Super Bowl rings and our two Stanley Cup championship rings. That YSU ring meant a great deal to me and I cherish it. Why? Because I knew how much it meant to Jim and how much he cared about our friendship."

Those random acts of kindness off the field make their way onto the playing field because Tressel made sure his players, coaches, and everyone else around the program always fostered those feelings

(Left to right) Rob Sims, A.J. Hawk, and Nate Salley take a rest on the bench during photo day of their senior season. The three players were leaders for Tressel, who epitomized the "family" concept.

inside them. A.J. Hawk was a linebacker for the Buckeyes from 2002 to 2005. A two-time All-American, he eventually became the No. 5 overall pick of the Green Bay Packers in the NFL Draft in 2006, signing a six-year, $37.5 million contract, led the team with 119 total tackles his rookie season and was third in the Associated Press Defensive Rookie of the Year voting. But you get the sense that he would have cashed it all in for one teammate in one important game against Michigan.

"My good friend Bobby Carpenter broke his leg on the opening kickoff of the Michigan game our senior year, and I didn't know what to say to him," Hawk said. "There really wasn't much you could say. I didn't even realize Bobby was off the field until two plays after he was gone, just because it happened so fast. He was limping on his own and limped off the field, then I looked in the huddle and realized he wasn't there and saw him on the sidelines. When the defense came off the field, I went right over to Bobby and asked him what happened and he said something was wrong, something was broken and he couldn't go anymore. I was almost speechless because I felt so bad for him, knowing it was our senior year and we were playing Michigan."

Hawk said he couldn't imagine how tough it was for Carpenter to have worked all year long for that big game and then break his leg on the first play. Carpenter was in tears, not as much because of the pain of his injury, but because of the disappointment of not being out on the field with his brothers in one of the biggest games of his life. "We all felt bad for Bobby because we all cared about him. But he knew we had to focus on our task at hand. Yet, there was Bobby on the sidelines on his crutches cheering us on. All I can say is that we won that game for him."

Archie Griffin drew similarities between Tressel's level of caring and the caring that Griffin's coach, the legendary Woody Hayes, displayed. "A player has to know that his coach cares about him, and I think the players here know that Jim cares about them," he said. "I knew that Woody cared about me and what I was going to do not only on the football field, but what I was going to do in my life. When you have that kind of caring and concern, it's everlasting."

Maurice Hall, a running back from 2001 to 2004, said that Tressel's philosophy of caring was something he wasn't accustomed to seeing. Hall, who was a quality running back and an exceptional student, was earning his master's degree while

MAURICE HALL

Position: Running Back

Hometown: Columbus, Ohio

Years Played: 2001–2004

Career Highlights: Hall was a solid team player during his four years at Ohio State. In OSU's 2002 championship season, he scored the winning touchdown in a close contest against rival Michigan.

conducting summer football camps at Ohio State's Woody Hayes Athletic Complex now that his athletic career is over. He was recruited by former Ohio State head coach John Cooper. Hall said that he had great respect for Cooper, but that Cooper let a lot of his assistant coaches coach the players.

"I'm not saying that's right or wrong," he said. "That's just how he did things. Coach Tressel was totally different in that aspect. He was more hands-on and I think that's the thing that stuck out with everybody. He encouraged all of us to know and care about everybody on the team, no matter who they were. If they were a starter, a walk-on, or the water boys and managers. That's something that hadn't been going on previously."

Tressel instituted a penalty if a player didn't know someone's name, their positions, hometown, or jersey number. Tressel would put a player on the spot, and if the player didn't know, he had to run. Of course, no one wanted to run, so during preseason camp, players made a point to go around introducing themselves so that they knew everyone from the superstars to the walk-ons. "That was something that allowed us all to become closer as a team," Hall said. "And because we came closer as a team and really cared about each other, we felt more comfortable with each other and working with each other in practice and in games. That, in turn, made us a better team."

Dan Kopp, a former YSU equipment manager who was named director of football operations for the Penguins in 2007, knew all about Tressel's level of caring, and it was reiterated during a trip to Columbus. "I remember going down to Columbus to visit Coach Tressel," Kopp said. "We went into one of the meeting rooms just to talk and visit and there was a quote by Coach Tressel's

"There was a quote by Coach Tressel's dad, Lee, on the wall, and it read, 'People won't listen to you until you they know how much you care about them.'... It was pretty simple, but pretty powerful."

dad, Lee, on the wall, and it read, 'People won't listen to you until they know how much you care about them.' I always had known how much of a caring person Coach Tressel was, but reading that quote, it was pretty simple, but pretty powerful."

Mark Snyder, who coached with Tressel at Youngstown State and Ohio State before being named head coach at Marshall in 2005, said the measure of caring that he witnessed at Youngstown State in 1993 was an experience he has never forgotten. It was a magical year for the Penguins, who were playing in their third consecutive Division I-AA national championship. They were playing against Marshall for the third straight year. YSU had lost to the Thundering Herd on a last-second field goal the previous year. But going into this game, Snyder said that he felt something special.

"We were out at our hotel having our last team meeting the night before the game and before the seniors got up to talk for the very last time, Dr. [Patrick] Spurgeon, our team doctor, talked about love," Snyder said. "Doc stood up and said, 'Love is the total and absolute giving of oneself with enthusiasm and joy that separates the exceptional from the excellent. This giving becomes the highest expression of love. If we hope to reach the top of the mountain, all of us must happily present the gift of our love through the absolute giving of ourselves to our comrades on the journey. This love is the hallmark of champions.'"

After that, each senior got up and spoke for about 30 seconds each. "It was the most emotional outpouring of love and caring I've ever felt in my professional life," Snyder said. "Then, and still to this day, it was something I'll never forget and it will always be etched in my brain. Guys were crying and I was bawling like a baby. The hugs that were going on and just the love, it was moving. It was powerful."

Following that emotional meeting, Snyder went back to his room and told his wife, "Honey, Marshall is probably more talented than us, but we're going to win tomorrow." "I told her, 'I just went

69

through the most amazing meeting I've ever been in.' She didn't understand and I don't think she still understands. It was unfathomable. The average person couldn't even fathom what went on in that room. It was something I'll never forget for the rest of my life," Snyder recalls.

Youngstown State dominated Marshall on its own field, jumping out to a 17–0 lead and holding the Thundering Herd to a 17–5 final score. "It was a great feeling winning a national championship at Ohio State, and there was some great love there, too," Snyder said. "All great teams have it, but I have never since felt that love like I did that night."

Tressel's caring extends far beyond the football field. He talks about the emails he receives on a daily basis from American soldiers who are Ohio State supporters. One email he received was from a soldier in Iraq whose wife was from Dayton, Ohio and had received her master's degree from Ohio State.

"He just wanted us to send her a little email because she was a little lonely during the holidays and she loved the Buckeyes, and we were able to do that," Tressel said. "Anything we can do to let the people…that are serving our country know that we appreciate them and we wouldn't be able to be doing this today if it weren't for them…. We owe a lot to them."

He tells the story of a group of soldiers who came to Columbus with their families during their short time on leave, just for the opportunity to watch their beloved Buckeyes practice.

"We had a number come over right before they were going to deploy," Tressel said. "I'm not sure my first choice, if I was home on five-day break from Iraq, would be to run over and watch practice, but that just shows you it's bigger than us."

It is a lesson that he aims to teach his players every day.

8 Grace in Adversity

There is no shortage of life-changing events that came out of Tressel's culture of caring. Former Ohio State defensive back Antonio Smith was one of the many individuals whose lives changed for better because of their relationships with Tressel.

His is a story of tremendous inspiration. A walk-on from nearby Columbus Beechcroft High School who was on academic scholarship through the Young Scholars Program, Smith worked hard in the classroom and on the field. In his senior year, he not only earned an athletic scholarship, he also earned a starting spot for the first time. He started in all 12 games, finishing second on the team with 71 tackles.

Smith ended his senior season as a consensus first-team All-Big Ten performer and was a semifinalist for the Thorpe Award, which is given to the top defensive back in the country. He also earned the 2007 Big Ten Outstanding Sportsmanship Award and was voted the Most Inspirational Player (the Bo Rein Award) by his teammates. He graduated with an engineering degree and, to cap off his amazing career, he signed a free agent contract with the Indianapolis Colts.

Every year, Smith said, Tressel asked each player to write down his short- and long-term goals. The goals ranged from things players wanted to accomplish on the football field to off-the-field goals. When Smith met with Tressel at the end of Smith's third season to discuss his future, Tressel asked the player if one of his goals was to earn an athletic scholarship. It was.

"The spring going into my fifth season, I had another meeting with Coach Tressel and he pulled out the goal sheet," Smith recalls.

"He said, 'Remember that goal you set about you earning an athletic scholarship? Well, that time has arrived.' It was a great feeling for me, knowing that all of my hard work, determination, and discipline finally paid off. And Coach Tressel is great at guiding young men from where we are to where we want to be not only in football but in life, religion, and in our family lives."

Tressel remembers that day clearly. "Antonio was one of those guys that had so much confidence in himself that he didn't care what anyone else thought," he said. "He knew what he was capable of and he had a great handle on what it would take—and he didn't care how long it would take. In this day and age, people use the word *persistence*, and what's missing in some young people's concepts about persistence is their patience. They persist for 20 minutes and think that's persistence.

"Antonio didn't care how long it was going to take. He didn't care that it was going to take him four or five years to get a scholarship or four or five years to be a starter, and he didn't care about guys being recruited each year and put right in front of him without them even being here a day. That didn't bother him because he had great confidence in his ability and there was no way he was going to stop. And here he is now a member of the Indianapolis Colts and a former starter at Ohio State, with his degree in engineering. Who would have thought that six or seven years ago?"

Those who know Tressel know that it doesn't matter what one's role is within the program. He endeavors to treat everyone the same: with respect and dignity. Over Tressel's 15 years at YSU, he developed a strong relationship with equipment manager John Murphy that remains solid. At a time in Murphy's life when his family needed a huge pick-me-up, Tressel was there.

It was December 3, 2005 and Murphy, a Youngstown Cardinal Mooney graduate, was watching his alma mater play in the state championship game in Canton, Ohio. (Mooney is the same school where Oklahoma coach Bob Stoops and his coaching brothers went to school.) Murphy received a call from his wife during the game. Their young son had a rash that concerned her, and she wanted to take him to the hospital. She took little Johnny to the emergency room, and Murphy left the game in the third quarter to meet his family there.

"I was sitting there in a waiting room while they're doing all of these tests on my son, and you couldn't imagine how scary [it] was for a child and the parents," Murphy said. "Then, the doctor came out and said, 'Your son's a diabetic.' We were in the hospital for the next five or six days, and Johnny's fever finally [broke]. We went and got a second opinion, but there was no doubt. He was a diabetic."

On Christmas Day of that year, the Murphys were visiting with family and friends in Youngstown when John Murphy noticed he had a message on his cell phone. It was from Bob Mansfield. Murphy hurriedly returned the call.

"John, there's somebody here that wants to talk to you," Mansfield said. A moment later, Tressel was on the phone.

"Now keep in mind, this is the day before Coach Tressel and the team [are] going to fly out to Arizona to get ready to play Notre Dame in the Fiesta Bowl," Murphy said. "Coach Tressel gets on the phone and says, 'Murph, I heard what's going on with Johnny. Well, you only get what you can handle. And the reason why you got that is because God knows you and Linda can handle that. You have to take care of that boy and you have to help find a cure for that disease.'"

Since then, the Murphys have been active in walk-a-thons in the Youngstown area to help raise money for juvenile diabetes and the American Diabetes Association. "When you work with Coach Tressel or if you're around him, he takes you to a higher level," Murphy said. "He challenges you, and if you're any kind of competitor, when you're challenged you're going to react to that challenge. Coach Tressel went out and found us a doctor in Columbus who works at the University as a pediatric endocrinologist and is on the cutting edge of diabetes care for juveniles."

The story didn't end there. Tressel made sure he could do something for little Johnny the next time he had the opportunity. That opportunity came a year later in December when the Murphys made another trip to Columbus to see their specialist.

As the Murphys were walking out of their appointment, Tressel and the football team were just getting off the bus. They had just come back from seeing *We Are Marshall* and were getting ready for practice to prepare for Florida in the national championship. Coach Tressel saw his opportunity to take a few minutes with Johnny.

"He sat with my son and talked to him for 20 minutes and told him he could do whatever he wanted to do," John Murphy said. "My son said, 'Can I go in that great big indoor place [the Woody Hayes indoor practice facility] and play catch?' Coach Tressel said, 'We don't start practice for an hour and a half. You can stay out there that whole time and play catch.' My son walked around the locker room, got an autographed football from all the players. He met Troy Smith, Ted Ginn Jr., and Anthony Gonzalez. Coach Tressel did that because once you work for him or play for him and give him your all, he'll always remember that and give you his all."

Tressel gave what he could to Jessica Moorhead, who died on March 6, 2003, at the tender age of 16, following a courageous four-year battle with leukemia. She was a junior at Youngstown Ursuline High School when she passed away.

While coaching at YSU, Tressel heard about Jessica's struggles and started to correspond with her, telling her to keep faith. Following Jessica's death, her mother established the Jessica Moorhead Foundation for Hope, an organization that "mobilizes Northeast Ohio businesses and citizens to ensure that the small but excellent Children's Care Center for Blood and Cancer continues to be available to local children and adolescents with cancer and chronic blood disorders."

The foundation also fosters programs that help meet patients' social and educational needs and involves patients and their families in community events.

Jessica's fight was so moving that Tressel included her obituary in Ohio State's *Winner's Manual*, along with the following letter that she wrote to him:

> "Do not lose the Courage, Hope and Faith you had in the past, which has a great reward. You must hold on, so you can do what God wants and receive what He has promised."
>
> —Hebrews 10:35–36
>
> There is a window in your heart through which you can see God. Once upon a time, that window was clear. Your view of God was crisp. You could see God as vividly as you could see a gentle valley or hillside. Then suddenly, the window cracked. A pebble broke the window. A pebble of pain and sadness. And suddenly God is not so easy to see. The view that you had seen so crisp had changed. You are puzzled. God wouldn't allow something like this to happen, would he? When you can't see him, trust him…Jesus is closer than you've ever dreamed.
>
> Please know that even though we don't always get the outcome that we want, God has the plan and everything will be okay. Don't allow this to shake your faith. I will see you all again someday in a better place than this. Trust in God and keep him close to you and I will be watching down on you."
>
> Love to All of You,
>
> Jessica

It was the last letter she ever wrote.

"I became aware of Jessica and her incredible struggle through one of our former players at Youngstown State who went to the same high school as Jessica and knew the family," Tressel said. "She was just an amazing, courageous young lady."

Jessica's mother, Jenifer, said he "got ahold of Jessica the year before he left to coach at Ohio State. Jessica was treated here in Youngstown when she was first diagnosed. About a year after she was diagnosed, she relapsed, which basically meant she had to have a bone marrow transplant and we had to go to Minnesota for that. We received so many cards and there were some that just stood out. Coach Tressel's was one of them. It was a personal letter from him basically telling her that he admired her courage and that he wished her the best and that he was here fighting for her. It came as a very big surprise."

Moorhead said she still meets people who remember her daughter's story. "I'm amazed at how so many people she touched, like a Jim Tressel," Jenifer said.

Jessica was diagnosed with leukemia in 1999, when she was in eighth grade. She was a cheerleader. "She battled for four years and it was amazing how the community rallied around her," Jenifer said. "There were blood [drives] and all kinds of fundraisers people started to help out."

Then came the day that Tressel's letter got into the hands of Jessica. "She was so rejuvenated when she got his letter," Jenifer said. "The well-wishes really meant a lot to her, but when something came like Coach Tressel's letter, well, that was really out of the ordinary because it came from nowhere and it was special. I can recall the day she got it. We used to cover her walls in her room with all of the cards that she would receive. So every day was a fun mail day. I remember her screaming, and it kind of scared me at first. She said, 'Mommy! Look who wrote to me!' She had that feeling like, *Wow! Somebody like Coach Tressel took the time to send me a card to try to make me feel better.* And it did make her feel better. It made a huge difference to her.

Knowing people were behind her made a huge difference in her life. It gave her the amount of hope that got her through many, many battles."

She recalled the times when Jessica really couldn't do too much because of her lack of strength, but she went back to school her sophomore year at Ursuline and was received with such a warm reception. She had been out of school since eighth grade, and when she did go back to Ursuline, she was only able to go back a half-day at a time. But she joined every organization she could. And she never missed a football game.

"What I've really enjoyed is that even after Coach Tressel left for Ohio State, Jon Heacock, who was the coach at Youngstown State after Tressel, kept the football program involved with the foundation and was extremely supportive as well," Jenifer said. "We have a fashion show every year, so for the past couple of years what I've done is I'd have a day of glamour for some of the girl patients. But one year, I decided I wanted to do something for the boys because they felt kind of left out of it. So I called Coach Heacock and asked him if we could come over to the football office with three of the boy patients who were in the fashion show. Coach Heacock was wonderful about doing it. The boys got a grand tour of the locker room, the weight room, and the stadium and had lunch with the players. While I was watching them, I just got this sense that those players were really, really special, like heroes to these patients and you could tell that some of what Coach Tressel had taught them was still with them. I think Coach Tressel laid the groundwork because he stood for something when he was at Youngstown State and he made sure that continued and his blessings are still here. And thanks to Coach Heacock, that caring and generosity among the coaching staff, players, and the entire community toward our foundation continues to this day."

9   Tyson's Courage

Tyson Gentry spent a lot of time at Ohio State's Woody Hayes Athletic Center. He was there when he didn't have to be. The building was his comfort zone. And the people inside it—his teammates, the Buckeyes' coaching staff, and everyone else affiliated with the program—were his extended family.

The game of football dealt Tyson a devastating and life-changing blow at the age of 20, leaving him paralyzed from the waist down. It would have been understandable if he had wanted to turn his back on the sport altogether. Yet Tyson felt no bitterness toward people, no bitterness about his situation. Through his own courage to persevere, he became a symbol of hope and inspiration for the Buckeye Nation.

"The thing that's amazing about Tyson is that...he truly believes that it's a blessing that he's had this adversity, which to me is mind-boggling," Tressel said. "But now that I've seen the inspiration he has been for so many people, it's special. And he's really just begun. He's going to touch so many lives for the rest of his life, and maybe a lot more than he would have as a backup receiver or a backup punter."

Gentry played high school ball out of Sandusky (Ohio) Perkins High School and then played at Ohio State from 2005 to 2006 as a punter and backup wide receiver.

Like so many young men from Ohio, Tyson's dream was to don the scarlet and gray and play for the Buckeyes. His father, Bob, is a former Buckeye himself. Football ran in the family.

"When it came to deciding where I wanted to play in college, my dad and my mom both supported me," Tyson said. "In fact, I initially made up my mind to go to Capital University [in Columbus, Ohio] and play football there. I could go there and play receiver. My sister went there, and I hadn't gotten that many offers from anyone else, but I knew I wanted to be in Columbus. Then Ohio State started talking to me about walking on there. Because Brandon Schnittker was on the team and brought it up to me that they were interested in having me walk on, I knew I couldn't pass that up. It was a dream for me to play for Ohio State."

So Tyson walked on as a punter at Ohio State. During his second season, Tyson was moved to wide receiver, a position he played and excelled at in high school. The Ohio State coaching staff loved Gentry's enthusiasm and effort and moved him to scout-team wide receiver during spring practices.

TYSON GENTRY

Position: Wide Receiver
Hometown: Sandusky, Ohio
Years Played: 2005–2006
Career Highlights: Gentry's story was so inspirational, he was a nominee his senior year for the 2008 FedEx Orange Bowl/ FWAA Courage Award. He suffered an injury during spring practice in April 2006 that left him partially paralyzed. Tressel, the coaching staff, and the players rallied around Gentry as a teammate after his injury.

"When we came back from spring ball after the [2006] Fiesta Bowl, the coaching staff asked me to switch to receiver permanently, so I was definitely excited about it because I loved playing receiver."

Tyson was content. He felt good about the progress he had made to earn the right to play wide receiver and he was proud of himself for all the hard work he put into the program to warrant such a reward.

Then came the day that changed his life forever.

The Buckeyes were conducting an intersquad scrimmage where the varsity and scout teams were combined and redivided to form even teams. As a scout player, he had not fully learned the Buckeyes' offense. Instead, his role was to run the opposing teams' offense to help prepare the varsity squad for its upcoming game.

Now that he had been promoted from the scout team, he was eager to play and to contribute to the offense. In the scrimmage, Tyson ran what he called a "dig route," in which the receiver runs straight down the field until he gets to a designated yardage, then breaks across the field parallel to the line of scrimmage.

"When I started going across the field, I got separation from the defensive back," Tyson remembers. "I got open, caught the ball, and went to tuck it and turn up field. As I went to tuck it, I started to fall."

At that point, the defensive back caught up to Tyson and dragged him down to the ground. "My neck snapped once I hit the ground and that's what caused the break. I'm almost positive that the ground caused my neck to break. I don't think it was the hit at all."

He sensed the seriousness of his injury immediately. It wasn't a "stinger," or something to walk off.

"I knew something was terribly wrong," he said. "I didn't even try to move because I couldn't move. I tried to move for about a second and realized that I wasn't going anywhere. I just lay there. I knew that it was pretty serious."

Tyson suffered a break of the C4 vertebrae. His football career was finished.

With the strength of his faith, and the strength of the Ohio State football family, Tyson and his immediate family became intent on using the accident as a platform to inspire others. But it wasn't easy.

Bob Gentry, Tyson's father, admitted, "As a family, we've been a very positive group all along. We've always been deeply involved with our three kids in everything they've done, from an academic standpoint to an athletic standpoint. In some of our discussions we'd had with them, we've told them that when anything happens, whether it's good or not so good, we will be there for them and be strong as parents.

"So Tyson's injury was really no different. If we're not there for the tough times and only there for the good times, then we're not the parents we think we are. Even though it is what it is, we have to deal with it and there's no reason to change our course in how we're dealing with it. We've been positive and we've had to make quicker adjustments than we've had to on some things because of the nature of what Ty's been dealing with, but that in itself is just part of handling things on the fly and we've all done that."

In the spring of 2007, while the Buckeyes were in the heart of spring drills, Tyson rolled his wheelchair into the Woody Hayes complex. He was exhausted, having just completed hours of physical therapy. But it had become a daily ritual that was as natural to him as brushing his teeth or combing his hair.

He just wanted to be around his extended family, and especially the man who was like a second father to him, Jim Tressel. When Tyson was "in the house," he made everyone feel at ease. Tyson refused to feel sorry for himself, or allow others to feel sorry for him.

"The whole experience of being around the program has been an awesome experience," Gentry said. "We're like a family and families go through periods where they have to face and handle adversity, but it makes you stronger as a family. It's definitely a privilege to be on the inside. There are times when I'll be sitting in team meetings and thinking about the fact that there are only so many people in the world that can say they've been behind closed doors with the coaches and the team and know what it feels like to be a part of this team and this program. And even with my injury, this whole experience has been great, to actually be able to say I played for him and was a part of this team."

When Bob Mansfield and Tressel became friends back in the 1980s, Tressel was the head coach at YSU and Mansfield was principal at an inner-city high school in Youngstown. Mansfield had been an educator and administrator in Youngstown for 25 years and Tressel valued his expertise. So Tressel added him to the staff at YSU as an academic advisor, and when Tressel was hired at Ohio State, Mansfield was right by his side. Tressel felt privileged to have a man like Mansfield associated with the program—a man who was a strong, positive influence on the players as it related to doing things right, on and off the field.

Prior to the accident, Mansfield was not well-acquainted with Gentry. But after the accident, the two got to know each other well. Mansfield had his own health issues to overcome. He had undergone a kidney transplant when he was in his fifties, and readily admitted that he was lucky to be alive. Mansfield saw the boy's strength in adversity, and acknowledged that it bolstered his own confidence.

"[Tyson] always had hope, and I don't know how you can live without hope," Mansfield said. "Coach Tressel spent a great deal of time with Tyson, and in his struggles, since day one, I never heard Tyson once say, 'Why me?' I always saw a smile on Tyson's face, even though I knew the rehab that he was going through was brutal.

"He was in the locker room all the time. He was in the team meetings. He was part of everything we did. And he was never excluded from anything. Tyson was a special guy because most people in those types of long-term, chronic struggles—and I saw it when I was on dialysis—most of them give up, get bitter, or lose their faith in God and humanity. They are just waiting for their end to come. But I've seen Tyson find other avenues. He wanted to go back to school and get his own apartment.

"His sister, Ashley, has been an angel for him and so have his parents. They are a phenomenal family and I bet they are tighter now than they were before, and they were a close-knit family before Tyson's accident. He had a lot of qualities that I wish I had. He had intangibles that, no matter what happens, will never be taken away from him."

What meant the most to Tyson during his injury and rehabilitation was how Tressel routinely visited him and shared stories with him about people Tressel met who had overcome similar injuries.

"To hear people tell me that I've been an inspiration to them really helps me," Tyson said. "But the bottom line is that there are definitely tough days where things are really going tough for me and I haven't been as upbeat as I have been in the past. That's just normal and obviously it's fine to feel like that, and I don't have a problem with that at all.

"My family—and my football family, as well—we all pretty much decided that even though this is not the greatest situation or the greatest story or the greatest thing that could've happened, there's really no reason to be sad or upset about it all the time. You're going to have a bad day, but you have to get up, keep going, and make the best of things. If you're going to sit there and be sad about it, then it's not going to get you anywhere. No matter what, you can never quit on yourself and you have to stay positive."

"I remember the first time I met Coach Tressel very vividly," Tyson reminisced. "The thing that impressed me most was it was our first day out at practice and I was warming up with the punters because I walked on as a punter. Coach Tressel came over and said, 'Hey, Gentry. How's everything at Perkins, and how's everybody in Sandusky doing?' I was blown away, because one, Coach Tressel knew who I was as a little old freshman punter walk-on, and two, he knew where I was from. That's the first thing I remember about meeting him, how caring he was about you whether you were a starter or a walk-on."

Tyson said he really appreciated the fact that Tressel still thought it was important for him to still be a part of the team and for him to know that he still had a place within the program, forever.

One of the traditions Tressel started at Ohio State was singing "Carmen Ohio," Ohio State's alma mater, with the student body after games.

"It was really neat, seeing the crowd and everybody looking at you, and the band right there playing in front of you, and knowing the team was behind you," Tyson said. "It was a special and awesome feeling and it was really neat to take part in that. And to still be able to do it even after my injury, that was something special.

"It's definitely sad to go through that and every now and then it gets me down," Tyson said. "But I would say that if I had the choice, I'd rather be around football enjoying it instead of staying away from it and not being a part of it. That would just not do me any good. It's great to be able to be around the team and still be able to get out there and enjoy it."

Tyson continued to take classes at Ohio State and started spreading his positive message to those who had faced similar situations. He spoke at schools, football camps, and to other organizations about the importance of keeping a positive attitude. He became a hero to many.

"I know how much I enjoy my life, how much I enjoyed being Tyson's age, and how much I enjoyed being in Columbus and being a part of the Ohio State football team, so I couldn't even imagine having that taken away," Bob Gentry said. "In spite of all that, it was hard to fathom that Tyson continued to go on with the positive approach. Here's a kid that basically had everything pulled out from underneath him, and he moved forward in a positive way. It makes the little complaints that we have every day in our lives so trivial."

"Every time you're around Tyson, you're just lifted up."

Bob Gentry said he remembers sitting with Tyson one day and hearing his son make a comment that stopped him in his tracks. They were watching a feature on a local television channel about former Ohio State linebacker Mike D'Andrea and his struggles with knee injuries and rehabilitation. He was a highly touted recruit out of high school, but his career was cut short because of his injuries.

After the television program was over, Tyson turned to his father and said, "What a really sad thing. Mike is such a good guy and such a good athlete."

"I was thinking, 'Here's a kid sitting in a wheelchair having been dealt the cards he's been dealt and here he is feeling bad for Mike,'" Bob Gentry recalled. It was a testament to Tyson's selflessness, as well as his own indomitable spirit.

Tressel said Tyson's best days are still in front of him. "He's going to make a difference in so many people's lives and he truly believes that the adversity that he's had to deal with is going to turn into a lot of great things and he believes that to the depths of his soul," Tressel said. "To me, that's inspiring in its own way. Every time you're around Tyson, you're just lifted up. We all get tired at times or we all feel down and feel sorry for ourselves, then you see Tyson and he doesn't feel that way. He's a difference maker."

Rosemarie Rossetti, Ph.D. is a powerful, internationally known speaker, trainer, consultant, writer, and publisher who walks her talk, as she has proudly shown. On June 13, 1998, Rossetti's life was irrevocably changed when a 3 ½ ton tree came crashing down on her. She was paralyzed from the waist down. But Rossetti has not let her tragic injury get her down. She took her story and her messages of hope and inspiration and shared it with others. Her program, "Just Like Riding a Bike: Coping with Change and Dealing with Adversity," is a transformational experience. Rossetti uses the lessons that she learned during her physical recovery to empower participants. It focuses on what motivates people to change their behavior, awaken their inner gifts, find meaning in their lives, and accomplish more to bring out the best in themselves. Participants leave revitalized and recharged, with restored hope, happiness, and an improved vision of their future.

Rossetti, who is the author of *Take Back Your Life!* and is Ms. Wheelchair Ohio 2004, wrote a moving story titled "Encouraging

Words Can Come From Unexpected Sources" about her first acquaintances with Tyson Gentry. Here is that story:

> A thank you card arrived in my mail last month from the family of Ohio State University football player Tyson Gentry. They thanked me for giving their son a copy of my book of inspirational articles *Take Back Your Life!*. The unexpected circumstances that led them to write this card may give you something to think about.
>
> On August 22, 2005, I had the opportunity to speak before the OSU Buckeyes football team and coaches. I shared the story about my spinal cord injury. I also shared lessons to live by to help them cope with change and deal with adversity, on and off the football field. I spoke about Adam Taliaferro, a Penn State football player who had a spinal cord injury during the September 23, 2000 game at Ohio State.
>
> At the end of my presentation, I handed out 8 ½ x 11 sheets of assorted colored construction paper and markers to each person in the audience. I asked them to write an inspirational message to the new patients with spinal cord injuries at the OSU Dodd Hall rehabilitation center. Each player signed his name and put his jersey number on his "Get Well" card. I explained that I would be taking the cards to Dodd Hall that evening and they would be displayed in the hallways. This would be a great way to boost the spirits of the patients, families, doctors, nurses and staff, especially during the fall football season.
>
> When the audience left the auditorium, my husband, Mark, as well as Coach Jim Tressel, his wife Ellen, and I began to read what the audience members had written.

At times, each of us read a verse from a card out loud and marveled at the sentiments. Tressel was amazed at the heart-felt language and artwork that his players had created. He shared personal stories with Mark and me about many of the players. You could see from his smile and the tears welling in his eyes that Tressel was very proud of what the players had expressed. Indeed, these Buckeyes offered inspiration and support to others whose lives had suddenly changed forever.

When I delivered the cards to Dodd Hall, they were treated with high regard. Several were framed, hung on the walls, and taped to the windows of the inpatient and outpatient facilities. They are still on display today. One of them reads, "Never give up no matter how much adversity you face. You can always overcome & beat adversity. A lot of people believe in *you*."

In April 2006, a Dodd Hall staff member photocopied that particular get well card and rushed it to the OSU intensive care unit. Why? Tyson Gentry, a 20 year old freshman on the football team was in intensive care. The OSU punter and receiver sustained a spinal cord injury during practice on April 14. He was taken to the OSU medical center for surgery on his neck. Later he was transported to Dodd Hall for rehabilitation, the same center where I spent five weeks after my injury in the summer of 1998. And who was the OSU football player that created that particular get well card? Tyson Gentry.

Never did I imagine how soon adversity would strike one of the players!

Ironic! The message he wrote was meant to be seen by a newly injured patient at Dodd Hall. Now he was that patient! One can only imagine what went through his mind when his get well card was delivered.

Today, I spoke to Gentry about his experience of receiving his card. He said that one of his nurses remembered that the card was at Dodd Hall and requested that the copy be sent. Gentry said, "When I saw the card, it was kind of weird and neat—a surreal experience! You never know what can happen. God throws things at you and you have to roll with the punches."

He told me that when I asked him in August 2005 to write the card, he remembered thinking about what to write. "I was clueless. I thought a few minutes. I had never been around a person with a spinal cord injury. I wanted to tell them to stay positive and fight through it. Funny how it happened the way it did."

Perhaps something I said in August 2005 will come to mind as he lay in bed thinking about his future. One of the lessons I explained during my presentation was to focus on a hopeful future, not on self pity. That lesson was taught to me by Christopher Reeve.

One year before my injury I was in the audience at Reeve's presentation in Columbus. Reeve spoke about the loneliness of his nights in the rehabilitation center and his thoughts of hopelessness. I remember him explaining how self pity is a trap that leads to deep depression.

When I was at Dodd Hall, I had a photo of Christopher Reeve, taken during his speech, mounted on the wall at the foot of my bed. I looked at it often during many lonely nights and tried to focus on how my life would have value again. As I focused my thoughts on a hopeful future, I began to feel encouraged about my recovery.

Today, Gentry has his get well card framed and sitting on the window ledge next to his hospital bed. Maybe this card can serve as his inspirational anchor for the next several weeks at Dodd Hall.

Each time I look at that thank you card from the Gentry family, I get an eerie feeling. Words of encouragement can come from a myriad of sources: people, books, articles, cards, and speeches. Given the chance to create a card, I wonder what I might have written before my injury. Maybe we should write a card to ourselves and give it to someone for safe keeping in case someday we need encouragement.

10 God Is Great

What's most important in Jim Tressel's life goes well beyond wins and losses or any individual coaching awards he has ever received. Alongside his family, it is his faith. And those around Tressel know that well.

"When it comes to Coach Tressel, he's a guy who has certainly led by example. It's clear that it's important to him for his players to do what is right and it's also clear that one of the reasons is because of his faith," said former Buckeyes defensive lineman Joel Penton.

In his senior year at OSU, Penton won the 2006 Humanitarian Heisman, given annually by the All Sports Association of Fort Walton Beach (Florida) to the college football player who combines the best exemplary community service with athletic and academic achievement. The trophy was named after 1996 Heisman Trophy winner Danny Wuerffel, who was executive director of Desire Street Ministries, a nonprofit faith-based organization established in a poor section of New Orleans (which was later destroyed by Hurricane Katrina). He also won the 2006 Rex Kern Award given by the Fellowship of Christian Athletes and spent time as community director for the Central Ohio Fellowship of Christian Athletes. Some said Penton had a career in the NFL. Instead, he joined a more "divine" team.

"For me, it wasn't a really difficult decision to leave football," Penton said. "I knew I was called to ministry. I love speaking and reaching out, and I just knew I was being called." Penton said there was something he read while at Ohio State that always stuck with him. "It was something by Jim Elliot that read, 'He is no fool who gives up what he cannot keep to gain what he cannot lose.' So, my thinking was, *What am I really losing by deciding not to pursue the NFL?* I'm not doing what typical college students do. And to do ministry, what am I losing? Not much. Just stuff that I can't keep, for one thing. Now, I'm gaining eternal significance which cannot be lost. You know it's time well spent. Even if I have to drive two hours and I only speak for 15 minutes, it leaves an impression that has an impact on young people's lives, and it has an impact on their eternity and, to me, that's something you can't compare to anything. It's worth 1,000 hours of my time because to make an impact on somebody's life is far greater than anything I can do for myself and it means experiencing a greater joy than I can express."

Tressel was among those who thought Penton could play in the NFL. He was also one who felt there was always something more than the fortune and fame of a professional career.

"Joel knew from day one when he got here what God had in store for him," Tressel said. "And there's no question that he knew if he became the best football player he could be, it would make his platform even larger to make a difference to people and have a podium to gain national attention from people. He could tell people what he was all about. I think there was no question going into his senior year that even though he was a guy [who] was going to be a part-time starter and rotated in our defensive front, he knew full well what he was going to ultimately do, which was to serve God. And he wasn't sure which way. He wasn't sure if he would pastor or go on to Bible school, but he found his passion with the Fellowship of Christian Athletes and he's doing a marvelous job."

Penton recalls a poem that had a profound impact on his life. He shares it with people any chance he gets. It is sometimes attributed to the late Roy Campanella, a Hall of Fame catcher for the Brooklyn Dodgers and one of the pioneers in breaking Major League Baseball's color barrier. Tragically, Campanella's career was cut short by an automobile accident in 1958 that left him paralyzed in and confined to a wheelchair.

The poem, entitled "A Creed for Those Who Have Suffered," reads:

A Creed For Those Who Have Suffered

I asked God for strength, that I might achieve.
I was made weak, that I might learn to humbly obey...
I asked for health, that I might do greater things.
I was given infirmity, that I might do better things...
I asked for riches, that I might be happy.
I was given poverty, that I might be wise...
I asked for power, that I might have the praise of men.
I was given weakness, that I might feel the need of God...
I asked for all things, that I might enjoy life.
I was given life, that I might enjoy all things...
I got nothing I asked for — but everything I had hoped for.
Almost despite myself, my unspoken prayers were answered.
I am, among men, most richly blessed!

Penton has read the poem at his speaking engagements as well as during the National Day of Prayer. "I use it all the time when I talk about how God answers prayers, despite him not always answering the way we want him to," he said. "The point is, he still answers prayers."

Former YSU wide receiver Herb Williams explained how he drew

HERB WILLIAMS

Position: Wide Receiver

Hometown: Boardman, Ohio

Years Played: 1990–1992

Career Highlights: Williams holds YSU's high mark for receiving yards in a season with 1,306 and is seventh in career receptions.

on his own faith to play football. "There are things that you are going to go through in life that may not be fair, but you have to persevere through it, and it makes you a stronger person because you know there was nobody in life tougher than Jesus Christ," Williams said. "He gave up his life and was betrayed by the people that he loved. So if Jesus could persevere through life, why can't I? So that's how I applied that while I was playing at Youngstown State."

Former YSU equipment manager Dan Kopp was born and raised in Youngstown, the son of a high school football coach. His father and Tressel were good friends, and Tressel formed a strong bond with the entire Kopp family. Faith was something they shared.

"Being Catholic, I was raised with great faith and belief," Kopp said. "And I liked that Coach Tressel always had some involvement with the Fellowship of Christian Athletes because I hadn't heard of that group before I started helping out at YSU. Coach would always have someone from FCA speak to the players, which is why something he said at the end of every game stuck with me then, and it still sticks with me. Coach Tressel would always say, after a game, win or lose, 'Remember who you are, worship somewhere, and spend time with your loved ones.'"

Roy Hall, an Ohio State wide receiver from 2003 to 2006, was an underrated receiver as a Buckeye because there were two high-profile receivers ahead of him: Ted Ginn Jr. and Anthony Gonzalez. Hall was much better than people realized and, in 2007, he was drafted to the NFL by the Indianapolis Colts. (And for the trivia buffs—Hall went toe-to-toe with LeBron James in high school basketball.) Even during his years as a Buckeye, Hall knew how important his faith would be in his life.

"You have to have faith and belief in God. It doesn't matter what you do in life," Hall said. "Coach Tressel is a Christian man, and a majority of our team was. Putting God first in all situations was important. A lot of guys go through injuries and other setbacks and they lose perspective on what's really important in their lives. What's most important is faith and belief in the Lord above."

Mike Peterson said that on Thanksgiving Day every year, he likes to call people who have been instrumental in his life to thank them for the impact they have made. "I called Coach Tressel

ROY HALL

Position: Wide Receiver

Hometown: South Euclid, Ohio

Years Played: 2003–2006

Career Highlights: Hall is a perfect example of *Winner's Manual* principles at work. He caught just 13 passes for 147 yards his senior year in 2006 but worked hard and had outstanding workouts leading up to the 2007 NFL draft, in which he was selected by the Indianapolis Colts in the fifth round.

one Thanksgiving and said, 'J.T., I want to thank you, not so much for the things you've done but for the fact that you allowed God to use me in my life. Because of that, I am where I am today.'

"He has instilled in me the expectations that I will win and succeed in anything I do. And it doesn't mean I'll be successful today, but the fact that you will get back up if you've been knocked down and that you'll get back in the game and you will be successful. The world may not understand that. They may not understand your principles and your attitude or your commitment or why you would go overboard and try to help someone that you may not even know or that it may put you in harm's way. But in Coach Tressel's world, God expects that of us, life expects that of us and we should expect that of ourselves.

"Millions of people can love Coach Tressel because he's won national championships and he's a winning coach, but I love him every time I look at my daughters and I see what he has helped me to build, how God has used him to strengthen me."

11 Buckeye Pride

When asked how proud he was to be a Buckeye, former Ohio State offensive lineman T.J. Downing paused for a moment, then said, "I have scarlet and gray in my blood." Downing was a dependable lineman who got the job done every time he stepped onto the field. In Downing's senior season in 2006, he earned first-team All–Big Ten honors. He is the son of Michigan All-American center Walt Downing, who played professionally for San Francisco and was a member of the 49ers team that defeated the Cincinnati Bengals in Super Bowl XVI.

T.J. Downing said he didn't recognize the privileged position he was in as a Buckeye. "I think my first two years at Ohio State I took for granted," he said. "I wasn't playing, I wasn't really noticed by the public as an Ohio State player. So being grateful to be a Buckeye really didn't hit me until my sophomore year when we played Michigan. We were big-time underdogs and no one gave us a chance to win. Michigan was undefeated at the time, they were trying to go play for a national championship if they beat us. And that was the first game I ever started in the Shoe.

"When we beat Michigan in the Shoe, that's when it all hit me, the meaning of being a Buckeye," Downing said. "The pride that you have wearing that Ohio State emblem, you take it for granted sometimes when you're red-shirted and you don't feel like you're important and you feel like the coaches don't give a damn about you. But when you get out there and you're representing Ohio State, it's such an honor. Winning that game is still with me. It's probably one of the greatest sports moments of my life."

Downing recalled the memories of being in the locker room at Ohio Stadium before a game. Twenty minutes before kickoff, the offense sat on one side of the locker room and the defense sat on the other. Offensive coordinator Jim Bollman would address the offense. "He would never say, 'Hey, we gotta go out there and score this amount of points' or 'We gotta hit 'em in the mouth,'" Downing recalls. "He would say, 'I want each and every one of you to look at yourselves and just be thankful that you're here in this position, because you can't even imagine how many other people are out there that would kill and die to be in your position.'"

A.J. Hawk had a great career at Ohio State that catapulted him to the No. 5 overall pick in the 2006 NFL draft. Things may have been a lot different if Ohio State hadn't "taken a chance" on him, as he puts it. Surprisingly, Ohio State was the only major Division I college to offer him a scholarship. Hawk had some mid-major offers from Mid-American Conference schools. There was a reason. "It was a good thing that I committed to Ohio State the July of my senior year because the first game of my senior year in high school, I got hurt. But Ohio State was good to me and they never, never acted like they were going to pull the scholarship.... If they did, I don't know where I would have gone. I think coming from a program like Ohio State where you learn so much about life, that tradition helped prepare me for my future— whether it was in the NFL, or as a lawyer, an accountant, an engineer,

A.J. HAWK

Position: Linebacker

Hometown: Centerville, Ohio

Years Played: 2002-2005

Career Highlights: Hawk was a two-time All-American for the Buckeyes. During his senior year in 2005, he won the Lombardi Award, which is given to college football's most outstanding lineman or linebacker. Hawk was the fifth overall pick in the 2006 draft by the Green Bay Packers. In his rookie season, he led Green Bay in tackles with 119 and finished third in the Associated Press Defensive Rookie of the Year voting.

or a teacher. I was really respectful and proud of where I came from in high school, and then getting to go to a place like Ohio State with Coach Tressel was unbelievable for me."

Dr. John Geletka, Tressel's good friend and agent from Youngstown, said Tressel always wanted to become the head coach at Ohio State, subconsciously. Tressel never publicly, or even privately, mentioned it. Tressel was an assistant there in the '80s under Earle Bruce. During Tressel's 15 years at Youngstown State, talk at OSU would occasionally turn to Tressel, at some point in his career, being the head coach of the Buckeyes.

Whenever critics started to call for Cooper's removal, Tressel's name would surface, at least in the local media. And when members of the media would ask Tressel about the rumors, he would always answer, "I've never talked about a job that wasn't open."

But then, that job became open.

"When Ohio State fired John Cooper, I was in Florida," Geletka said. "I called Jim and said, 'Well, your job's available, what are you going to do?' He said, 'You think they're going to call me?' I said, "Hell, no. They're not going to call you. You already turned down five or six jobs.' Geletka said one of those jobs Tressel turned down while he was at Youngstown State was the University of Miami job, vacated by Jimmy Johnson. "The Miami job was the job I thought he definitely should've taken," Geletka said. "But what did I know?"

Geletka had also encouraged Tressel to accept the head coaching position at Marshall, a school that was stacked with quarterback Chad Pennington and wide receiver Randy Moss, two future NFL players. And since Marshall was playing in the Mid-American Conference, Geletka felt Tressel would have probably won 20 games before he lost his first game. "I told Jim he needed to go to a Division I school first and that he would not get to Ohio State from Division I-AA Youngstown State," Geletka said. "Well, evidently, I was wrong. He got the Ohio State job and the rest—well, we know the rest."

The Horseshoe in Columbus may have been a slightly different venue than Stambaugh Stadium at Youngstown State, but Tressel was the same coach both places, well-prepared and focused.

That's when Geletka finally got paid. "Jim's first contract was pretty much cut and dried because he was getting a big job and he was going to make six times what he made at Youngstown State," Geletka said. "But the first thing we put in his contract was, if he won the national championship, he got to redo the contract again. A year after he got to Ohio State, we had to renegotiate his contract because he won the national championship. That's when I told Jim, 'You could retire from Ohio State, run for the U.S. Senate, win handily, and you could be president of the country someday.' He just looked at me and said, 'You're nuts.' I said, 'What do you mean? A movie actor has been president. A peanut farmer has been president. Why couldn't you be president?' He just laughed and walked away. But I can tell you, he loves his job more than anyone and he loves The Ohio State University."

Former defensive back Antonio Smith took one very valuable lesson from Tressel. The coach emphasized to his players that if they reached short of a goal, it may have been disappointing, but there was always a chance at redemption.

And when the Buckeyes lost to Florida in the 2006 national championship, the players and coaching staff were disappointed. But they had a chance at redemption and they worked hard during the off-season and got back to the national championship game the next year, this time against LSU. And even though the Buckeyes lost that game as well, it only made the team strive for redemption even more.

That was the case with Smith. "One of the greatest moments for me at Ohio State, other than being a red-shirt freshman when we won the national championship in 2002, was when I returned an interception for a touchdown in the Horseshoe my senior year against Penn State at the end of the game," he said. "It was a sloppy, dirty game and the score was pretty close. In the fourth quarter, my teammate, Malcolm Jenkins, intercepted a pass and took it for a touchdown and that put us ahead. Then, I was able to get an interception and returned it for a touchdown, and that put the game away for us."

The year before, the Buckeyes went to Happy Valley and lost to Penn State. The fans there had what they called a "white out": everyone in the stands wore white. It was a disappointing loss for the Buckeyes, though Smith had returned an interception for a touchdown in the effort.

The next year, Penn State had to travel to Columbus. It was the Buckeyes' chance for redemption. And all the fans in the Horseshoe had a "scarlet out." In that game, Smith returned an interception for a touchdown, just like he had done in that loss at Penn State the year before. But this time, his interception return was on his home field, and in front of his home fans.

"When I caught the ball and ran to the end zone, it was just a sea of scarlet," Smith said. "It was a great feeling. It was a beautiful thing. To me, that was a proud moment as a Buckeye."

However, Smith said his greatest moment being a Buckeye wasn't a game that the team won, or even something he achieved on the field. "My proudest moment as a Buckeye came when I graduated in June 2007 with an engineering degree," he said. "That's my greatest achievement, because being able to maintain a 3.1 grade-point average was hard. I had to balance the rigors of my schedule with labs and homework, and still had to perform on the field as well, with practice, games, and travel. It was definitely tough, but I like challenges and it was worth it. Academically, my mindset was that I was going to take advantage of every opportunity because initially that's what I went to Ohio State to do. My family is very proud of me for what I've done and the person I've grown to become. Going to Ohio State and being part of that tradition and having that respect not only carries over into the next level, it carries over into people's lives."

Downing gave the most poignant description of why he was proud to be a Buckeye. "When I look back, all I can say is that I'm just so grateful that I had the opportunity to play for a university like Ohio State and to be able to have that name carried with me the rest of my life," he said, sounding very reflective, even spiritual. "When I die, people are going to say, 'Hey, that was T.J. Downing. He used to play for Ohio State.' They're going to say, 'That guy was an Ohio State Buckeye.'

"I'm also very grateful for Ohio State and what the university and the program have done for me. When you think about all the great players who have...come through here, it's mindboggling. And to be able to put your name up with these guys is something you just have to be so grateful for. If you don't get down on your hands and knees and thank God for the opportunity he's given you at Ohio State, well, that's doing a disservice to this program and all the people who were part of this program."

Downing grew up in the Cleveland area, so he saw first-hand how much influence the program had in the area. "The Cleveland area,

Northeast Ohio, and the entire state of Ohio is huge for us," Tressel said. "If we are going to have a huge football team, I'm sure there are going to be some guys from Cleveland who make an impact, guys from Cincinnati, and throughout the entire state. One of the things we've always said is the thing that gives us a chance at Ohio State to have a good program is that the high school football in Ohio is outstanding, the high school coaching is excellent, the game is important to the people in Ohio. When you grow up in Cleveland and you are watching the Browns and you are watching the Buckeyes, you get excited about becoming a football player.

> "It's bigger than just us playing and coaching today."

"Ohio State is special," Tressel said. "What we try to understand about that is that it's a privilege to play at Ohio State. It's a privilege to coach at Ohio State.

There's been excellence from the beginning of time at Ohio State. There's a certain responsibility you have to uphold with that fine tradition. It's bigger than just us playing and coaching today. Our alumni are huge all over the country. We graduate thousands of people every year and they disburse all over the land and all over the world to make a difference....

"Ohio State football is [one way] that they get to hold onto their collegiate experience, by watching and cheering," he said. "That's a responsibility. But I think the biggest lesson you try to understand at Ohio State is that it's bigger than you."

12 The Right Attitude Means Everything

Malcolm Jenkins started the 2008 season as a four-year starter for the Buckeyes and ended it as an All-American and Thorpe Award winner, which goes to the nation's top defensive back. More importantly, he was also one of the leaders on the team. In his freshman season in 2005, he had established himself as a quality impact player on and off the field who was well-liked. Whenever the team needed a jolt of positive attitude, Jenkins was always there to give it.

"Malcolm was always full of spirit and always had the right attitude," Tressel said. "When a freshman goes out there and he's just bubbling and showing unbelievable confidence through his positive attitude, if he's scared, you don't know it. If he's homesick, you don't know it. If he wasn't sure whether or not he could play, you don't know it. Malcolm was filled with so much spirit and enthusiasm and energy and a positive attitude that he was acting like a veteran. And he was contagious to the rest of the guys."

Jenkins said he hated preseason camp as a freshman, but when he stepped on the field, he tried to have as much fun as possible. He wouldn't stop talking, he'd be in his teammates' faces trying to get them pumped up. "That got me through camp and that got the coaches to look at me, and I ended up starting as a freshman," Jenkins said. "When you're tired and you don't feel like doing things, or the team needs a boost, the right attitude can take you a long way. You might not have the most talent, but your attitude is the thing that will get you noticed by coaches. That's what happened to me. Whenever you do anything with enthusiasm and a positive attitude, you'll perform at a much higher level."

In Jenkins' freshman year, Ohio State had a solid group of veteran players with A.J. Hawk and Bobby Carpenter. Jenkins earned their respect with his positive attitude that exuded confidence but not cockiness. It was his attitude that allowed him to join a defensive group that was well-developed but always looking for someone to step up and help out. Defensive back Dustin Fox had just graduated, so the defense was looking for a capable starter in the secondary. "We were looking for some help as a defense, and with the attitude Malcolm showed and the confidence he carried, I think there was no question that he wasn't going to wait at the back of the line—and that made the difference," Tressel said.

Archie Herring's positive attitude turned him into one of YSU's most efficient running backs. Just before the start of the 1989 season, Herring's junior year, and during two-a-days, Tressel came knocking—literally—at Herring's door. Herring answered. "I was in my dorm room at Kilcawley Center and Coach Tressel showed up," Herring said. Herring opened the door and greeted Tressel. Then Tressel said, "I need to talk to you." Herring wasn't worried that he was in trouble because he didn't get into any.

They walked down to the end of the hallway and sat down on a couch. Then Tressel laid it all out for Herring: "Now, this is your decision and I know you've been really working hard to play defensive back and you're fighting for a spot and you could possibly end up starting. But I need you to come over and play running back. You don't have to make your decision now. I just want you to think about it. The team needs you, and I think we can take it to another level if we had you at running back because you bring something to the table that some of the other tailbacks don't have, and we really need you."

YSU had come off a rough '88 season offensively, and Tressel felt the team could be more explosive in '89 with a few personnel moves.

One change was moving Florida native Lorenzo Davis from running back to wide out. (That move paid dividends for Davis, catapulting him into the NFL with the Pittsburgh Steelers.) But moving Davis to a receiver position left Tressel with just one running back. "We didn't think for as much as we wanted to run the football that we could afford to only have one running back," Tressel said.

Herring understood the route Tressel wanted to go. "I thought about it long and hard and I thought about everything Coach Tressel imparted on me about being a team and being family," Herring said. "He built the Youngstown State program into a family. So my thought was, *I don't want my family to go down. I have an opportunity to help the family,* and I went ahead and made the switch, and it was probably the best thing for me in my career."

He led YSU in rushing that season with 1,095 yards and 12 touchdowns and helped the Penguins to a 9–4 record and a playoff appearance. "There's no question it was because of Archie's positive attitude and maturity that he had the kind of year he had and, quite frankly, the kind of year we had as a team," Tressel said. "We felt like Archie, with his ability and speed—he was a 4.3 40 guy—that if he would be willing to move from defense to offense, we could be a better team. And thank goodness Archie had the maturity.... It wasn't about what he wanted or needed, it was about what the team wanted and needed."

Oftentimes, keeping the right attitude during adversity leads to confidence. That was the case with Ohio State running back Chris "Beanie" Wells during his freshman season in 2006. Wells' first year was met with mixed reviews. He wasn't the featured back at the time (it was fellow Akronite Antonio Pittman), but he showed glimpses of greatness. He was the top running back recruit in the country coming out of Akron Garfield High School, the same school as former Ohio State defensive back and NFL standout Antoine Winfield.

Fans in Columbus were expecting a lot from Wells. During his freshman year, he finished with 576 yards on 104 carries and seven touchdowns and fans had a lot to be excited about when it came to this incredible talent. The only problem was, he fumbled way too much for Tressel's liking, or the fans'. Wells was benched several times for

CHRIS "BEANIE" WELLS

Position: Running Back

Hometown: Akron, Ohio

Years Played: 2006–2008

Career Highlights: Wells set a school record for most yards by a sophomore with 1,609 in 2007. He also set a school record for most rushing yards against rival Michigan with 222. He missed three games in his junior season because of a foot injury, but still rushed for 1,197 yards.

turning the ball over, but he was always given the chance to redeem himself. And he did in a win against Michigan in the 2006 regular-season finale. Wells lost a fumble at a crucial time in that game, but Tressel stuck with him, and the back eventually scored on a 52-yard touchdown that proved to be the game-winner.

The following year, Wells was a completely different running back. He was more reliable, he was confident. He was virtually unstoppable, rushing for 1,609 yards and 15 touchdowns to help the Buckeyes reach the national championship game. His name started to get thrown out for Heisman consideration.

"I had those problems my freshman year dealing with fumbling the ball, but I always made sure that when I did mess up, miss a block, or fumble, I kept a positive attitude," Wells said. "As a freshman and playing at the college level, I was always thinking that if I messed up in a game, I was going to get benched and never play again. Coach Tressel wasn't that way. He was the type of guy that always gave me a second chance because he knew what I could do, so he would put me back on the field. That's why I knew, as long as I kept a positive attitude, I would get that second chance."

Jim Dennison is a well-respected coach among the Ohio coaching circles. A former head coach at the University of Akron from 1973 to

1985, he gave Tressel his first coaching job—as a graduate assistant for the Zips shortly after Tressel graduated cum laude with a bachelor's degree in education from Baldwin-Wallace College. Tressel was a four-year varsity letter winner and won all-conference honors as a senior.

"I don't think there's any question that when Jim was coaching with me at Akron in his early days and in his first coaching job, he exhibited the same qualities as he does right now because our slogan at Akron was 'Win with PMA: Positive Mental Attitude,'" Dennison said. "I believe that a positive mental attitude is the most important thing in working with young people today—in everything we do—because attitude will help us in handling the problems that we come across in everyday living.

"I get letters, and I sure Jim does too, every single day from people who are going through adversity, people who are battling cancer, people who have gone bankrupt, people that have lost children, lost parents, and all kinds of other setbacks and tragedies that one might face in their lifetime," Dennison said. "I'll get calls and letters and emails from those people who say that the positive mental attitude they had gave them hope to keep moving ahead. They tell me that their positive attitude keeps them strong. That's why I still coach, and that's why Jim does the great job that he does. It's because we truly feel we still do make a difference."

Earle Bruce said, "[Tressel] coached for me for three years so I know a little bit about his ideas and philosophies, and I think he did a great job at putting them all to work and teaching them to the players. Attitude is more important than talent, because if a player has the wrong attitude, he's not going to help to stay successful. I can point to Maurice Clarett and many failures with bad attitudes. But I can point, too, to many great kids with great attitudes that played above themselves in big games like against Michigan or whoever the bowl game opponent might be. I can see kids with the great attitude for the game of football, the great positive attitude that they had....

"A good attitude is bigger than anything else in [determining] the success of a person, whether they're playing football or in life," Bruce continued. "Attitude, in my book, comes before talent because I've seen many kids with great talent never make it, and I've seen kids with some talent but a great attitude and they work hard, stay at Ohio State for five years and end up great human beings when they leave here."

Jeff Wilkins, a Youngstown State place-kicker from 1990 to 1993, retired from the NFL after the 2007 season following a successful 14-year career, most of them with the St. Louis Rams. He played in two Super Bowls with the Rams, beating the Tennessee Titans in 2000 and losing in 2002 to the New England Patriots.

> "A good attitude is bigger than anything else in [determining] the success of a person."

Wilkins never imagined he would have such a long and illustrious NFL career, or even make it to the NFL for that matter, when he was a freshman at Youngstown State. Heading into two-a-days Wilkins' freshman year, Youngstown State had another kicker in camp, Darren Morgan, who was the incumbent. The two competed against each other and Wilkins won the job.

In Wilkins' first game, he missed two field goals and was 1-for-4 in attempts in his first two games. "I felt like I wasn't helping the team and my confidence obviously was down," Wilkins said. "Here I was, a true freshman and I wasn't used to college. Coach Tressel called me to his office for a meeting and said, 'Jeff, you're still our guy. We went through two-a-days and you proved to me that you can do this.' That's when I got my confidence back. I started to believe in myself. I had such a positive attitude after that meeting with Coach Tressel and I just told myself I had to step up my game. From then on, I was able to keep the job and ended up having a pretty good freshman year."

Indeed, Wilkins ended up having an outstanding career at YSU. During his senior year, he made a school-record 66 field goals with a long of 54 yards, which was then a school record.

He took that same positive attitude into the NFL and in a position where he had to have confidence

JEFF WILKINS

Position: Place-Kicker

Hometown: Austintown, Ohio

Years Played: 1990–1993

Career Highlights: At YSU, Wilkins held career records for most points by a kicker (373), point-after kicks made (173), field goals made (66), and field goals attempted (98). He is YSU's most-accomplished NFL player. He enjoyed a 14-year career in the NFL, mostly with the St. Louis Rams, and played in two Super Bowls.

and a positive attitude or he was bound to fail. In high school, if a quarterback or running back throws an interception or fumbles the ball, he may have 20 or 30 more chances to vindicate himself and, by the end of the game, he can be the hero again. Kickers get one, two, maybe three kicks a game, so either they are the hero or the goat—there's no inbetween. In college, if a kicker misses a kick or two, he's not going to get kicked off the team. There may be some ill feelings for a short period of time among teammates and even coaches, but the kicker is still kicking the next week.

In the NFL, as Wilkins pointed out, a missed kick can cost you a job. "That's how I got my job with the San Francisco 49ers," said Wilkins. "San Francisco had Doug Brien and he was drafted in the third round and I was a free agent. He had a pretty good first year. But a few years later, he missed two game-winners in back-to-back weeks and was gone. Other than that, his stats were really good. It wasn't anything more than two kicks at critical times that cost him his job. If they were two kicks in the first quarter, he probably wouldn't have lost his job.

"Being a kicker is such a pressure position in the NFL and you can't afford to miss those important kicks," Wilkins continued. "You can miss a few here and there, but you better make a lot of good ones in between. I truly believe that one of the reasons why I lasted so long in the NFL is because of my freshman year at YSU and Coach Tressel helping me get my confidence back when I had lost it after just two games my freshman year. I kept a positive attitude and it helped keep me in the NFL for 14 years, which is a long time for a kicker."

13 Troy Smith

The relationship between Tressel and former Ohio State quarterback and 2006 Heisman Trophy winner Troy Smith developed into something very special during the course of Smith's collegiate career, especially during Smith's last two seasons. It wasn't until Smith's redshirt junior year that he turned things around and put himself in a position to make a run for the Heisman.

When did it all click for Smith? When did he realize the enormous potential he had? And when did he realize that he could change the course of his life by making the right decisions?

Smith said it clicked for him when he went back home during one break from school and saw his mother and his younger sister struggling. He realized that he needed to get them out of that difficult situation at home and into a positive situation where they felt comfortable with their everyday lives. It's what caused him to focus in college and that's what made him become a more responsible man his last two years at Ohio State.

"I had a meeting at my house in Cleveland with Coach Tressel and Mr. [Gene] Smith my redshirt junior year, and I realized that my sand in the hourglass was running out and that the straw was starting to break on the camel's back, so I had to grow up as a man," Smith said. "I left the meeting with those guys and they let me know that there was no more time to be playing around. They let me know that I had a chance to be the leader of this team, and when you have two distinguished men in front of you telling you their plan and what they have laid out for themselves, their livelihood, the university, and this whole state, you don't play around with that, and that's what pretty much changed it for me."

There is a small number of Tressel's players, from Youngstown State and at Ohio State, who will tell you that Tressel has a subtle way of getting a message across. He may go about it in non-traditional or not-so-noticeable ways, but he'll get his point across to a player. That was his approach with Troy Smith.

"Troy's redshirt junior year was Mr. [Gene] Smith's first year here at Ohio State," Tressel said. "Obviously, he and I had traveled a lot of miles leading up to that visit to see Troy and Troy had great support from [Glenville] Coach [Ted] Ginn [Sr.] and from a variety of people along the way. Troy had some experiences here at Ohio State, many of which were good, others that weren't. And I think he was right at that point where he was really starting to figure it all out.

"It was just great timing and I think there was a natural mesh between Troy and Mr. Smith because you had two guys from Cleveland, and Troy was at that point where he was really starting to feel confident about himself and like anything else, you never know which step is going to be a key one. I'm certain that Troy's redshirt junior year and his meeting with Mr. Smith was a key step."

When Gene Smith became the athletic director, he and Tressel hit it off right from the beginning. Tressel was happy knowing he had a boss who was a former coach, not to mention a Cleveland native who could be a resource when it came to handling Troy Smith. It wasn't football that afforded Gene Smith the opportunity to reach the professional success he achieved; it was academics and doing things right. So when Gene Smith became the Ohio State athletic director, he was very anxious to sit down with Troy.

"I remember talking to Gene once and saying, 'You know, I think it would be neat if Troy had one more voice in his ear,'" Tressel said. "Troy had lots of good voices, [like] Coach Ginn, [Ohio State quarterbacks coach] Joe Daniels, and all the people that made

Coach Tressel and Troy Smith are interviewed by ABC's Jack Arute after the Buckeyes' win in Michigan in 2006.

an impact on Troy. But one more voice would certainly enhance that."

Smith had some troubled times growing up. He spent time with a foster family while his mother tried to sort out her life. That instability at such a tenuous time in his life led to him making some bad decisions. He started the first two years of his high school career at perennial powerhouse St. Edward in Lakewood, Ohio, a suburb of Cleveland, but was expelled for reportedly throwing an elbow to the head of an opponent during a varsity basketball game.

Smith had played peewee football for the Glenville A's, so it made sense that he enrolled at Glenville High School after being dismissed from St. Edward. Ted Ginn Sr. was the longtime coach at Glenville, and his son Ted Ginn Jr. would become Ohio State's star wide receiver and later a first-round pick by the Miami Dolphins in the 2007 NFL draft.

Glenville may have been in a rough part of town, but the students strove for excellence in sports and in the classroom. With Ginn Sr. running things, student-athletes weren't given free rides. He was the perfect coach for Smith. In fact, Ginn Sr. was a man who was much like Tressel in that both wanted to see young men prosper well beyond their athletic accomplishments.

In Smith's senior year at Glenville, he threw for almost 1,000 yards, and with Ginn Jr. as his favorite target, the duo led the Tarblooders into the state playoffs. Both players solidified their places as legitimate Division I college prospects. The only problem for Smith was that he still carried a lot of baggage that didn't have anything to do with football. So, despite his talents, some programs harbored hesitation in offering Smith a scholarship. In fact, Smith accepted the last scholarship of Ohio State's 2002 football recruiting class.

Smith was still rough around the edges when he arrived at Ohio State and was red-shirted. He finally got a chance to hit the field a year later, playing in the Buckeyes' 2003 season opener against Washington. The redshirt year was a good thing for Smith; he had to earn respect and nothing was handed to him. He had to earn that respect from his teammates and especially the coaching staff. They wanted to see if he would mature and leave those bad habits behind, if he would develop into a quality student-athlete.

In 2004, Smith's sophomore season, he was installed as the backup to Justin Zwick. Zwick was highly touted coming out of powerhouse Massillon (Ohio) High School, but he hadn't developed into the prolific passer at Ohio State that he was in high school. He was still an efficient player and, more importantly, he was a stand-up individual and student-athlete.

Smith and Zwick were friends while they were teammates and competed against one another. They also respected one another. "When Troy took over the starting position, it was tough for me to handle at first because it was a thing where I was always used to starting my whole life and now, I'm not playing," Zwick said. "But I had to realize that it was the path my life was going to take at that time and I really didn't want to dwell on it. I just wanted to be able to help him and help the team. He was the same way.

"I remember going into the Texas game in 2005 with a lot of uncertainty," Zwick continued. "I didn't know how the rotation was going to work at quarterback and neither did Troy. As the game unfolded, I played the first couple of series and then Troy took over. I was able to get back in a little in the third quarter, but Troy eventually took over. When you look back, you see that you wished a lot of things could've been different. A lot of people will remember the fumble I had in the end zone late in the game and us trailing Texas in a close game."

JUSTIN ZWICK

Position: Quarterback

Hometown: Orrville, Ohio

Years Played: 2004–2006

Career Highlights: Zwick was the highest-rated quarterback in the nation coming out of high school. He was redshirted in his freshman season and became the starter the following season. He ultimately lost his starting job to teammate Troy Smith in 2005, but remained a steadfast teammate throughout his career.

The critics had blasted Tressel when he took Smith out in a crucial point late against Texas and put in Zwick. Zwick went in and fumbled after being pressured and the Buckeyes eventually lost the game and a chance at playing for the national championship. Zwick never complained about his limited playing time and was the model team player and student-athlete during his entire Ohio State career.

"People will remember that because it was the last play for us on offense," Zwick said. "But throughout that game, there were times when we just weren't able to take advantage of some of the opportunities we had. I've really learned over the past few years that God has a plan for us all and that was just how the plan was made and that's how things were supposed to go. You just have to learn from it. Not many people get to face those types of tough situations at a young age like we did, but those situations shaped us as young men and really I believe going through all the things I have really has made me into the person I am today."

Smith finally got his chance to start halfway through the year after Zwick was injured. Smith filled in admirably, winning four of the five games he started in 2004, the biggest of them against rival Michigan.

It appeared Smith was on his way to becoming a star for Ohio State and the future face of the Buckeyes' program, but indiscretions once again crept in and got him into trouble. He was suspended late in the 2004 season just before the Alamo Bowl against Oklahoma State University for breaking an undisclosed team rule. It was later revealed that Smith accepted $500 from a booster. His suspension also included Ohio State's 2005 season opener against Miami University of Ohio.

"Troy had fought through the issues when he had to miss that final game his redshirt sophomore year," Tressel said. "That was right about when Gene came here, and I had to explain to [Gene Smith] why Troy wasn't out there when we were going through spring drills and preseason drills. I had to explain why Troy wasn't going to get that chance to start in that opener his junior year. So there were some consequences and Gene was very willing to understand where we were on this long road and wanted to help in any way he could to help Troy finish strong."

Bob Mansfield, who became resident counselor/father figure to many of the players at Ohio State, developed a very strong allegiance toward Troy Smith. The players responded to Mansfield because he wasn't fake, and he didn't just tell them what they wanted to hear.

"I liked Troy as a person and as a young man, and I didn't even look at the athletic potential he had," Mansfield said. "I just thought he had that intelligence and charisma, and you could see that he had something special. He did have a little bit of an attitude and was a little rebellious, and at times he didn't want to believe in what was going on. I remember many times sitting in the locker room with him and telling him that he needed to trust Coach Tressel, and if he could trust the guy in charge good things would happen."

Mansfield said Smith would listen to him and was respectful, but he still got the sense that Smith was reluctant to follow his advice. "Troy was coming from the streets, so I could see that he didn't trust too many people," Mansfield said. "I told him, 'Troy, you have to trust Coach Tressel. You have to believe in something. You have to believe in somebody. You have to work hard and you have to compete. If you do that, things will work out for you.' And as he listened, you saw everything unfold in front of him. You saw him become more and more of a man.

"I remember Coach Tressel sitting with Troy in meetings while watching film and telling him that if he watched film and did all the little things, he could be a great quarterback someday," Mansfield said. "Coach Tressel told Troy if he didn't believe it, then it wouldn't happen. Then, you could slowly see the maturation process in Troy. If you listened to Troy in press conferences, he sounded like Coach Tressel. What Troy did was finally buy into the program."

During Smith's 2005 redshirt junior year, he put up impressive numbers for a part-time starter. He threw for 2,282 with 16 touchdowns and four interceptions and rushed for 611 yards and 11 touchdowns on 136 carries. His 162.66 passing rating was the fourth-highest of all quarterbacks in the nation that season.

Smith was instrumental in leading Ohio State to a 25–21 come-from-behind win at Michigan Stadium his junior year and also led the Buckeyes to the 2006 Fiesta Bowl, where he was named offensive MVP after leading Ohio State to a convincing 34–20 win against Notre Dame.

In Smith's senior season, he became a serious Heisman candidate. It started with Ohio State's 24–7 win at Texas, which avenged the loss to the Longhorns in Columbus a year earlier. Smith had locked up the Heisman Trophy, as far as Tressel was concerned, after Smith's gutsy performance in the Buckeye's 42–39 win at Ohio Stadium in 2006. It was a game that matched the No. 1 Buckeyes against the No. 2 Wolverines, and it was a Michigan team that many Ohio State followers felt was as arrogant as they had ever seen. The Wolverines had a quality team with preseason Heisman running back candidate Michael Hart, a strong quarterback in Chad Henne, and a nice receiver in Mario Manningham. But none of that mattered to Smith. He wasn't playing against Michigan as much as he was playing for his teammates and coaching staff, whom he loved.

"I'm at a loss for words right now," Smith said during the post-game press conference. "I was downstairs with my teammates and the overall feel of everybody is unparalleled. You wouldn't be able to understand it unless you ran the bases that we ran, ran the hills that we ran, pushed the sleds that we've pushed, played power ball. We've got a game called power ball, too, we play a lot. When that heat and that sun are beating down on your back in the summer, the commitment and the focus.... Focus was the key word for us today, and everybody focused in. Words can't express how I feel right now. I'll probably be wearing this smile for the rest of this week. I love every single one of my teammates with the deepest passion you can probably have for another person."

Meanwhile, in Tressel's mind, Smith's performance against Michigan (he was 29-of-41 for 316 yards and four touchdowns) was proof that his quarterback had come a long way.

"Well, I would think he clinched the Heisman Trophy. I don't think there'd be any question about that," Tressel told reporters during the postgame press conference. "I think he's the best player in college football."

When Smith was asked about the possibility that he might have clinched the Heisman Trophy after the Michigan win, he replied like Tressel himself would have. "I think the Heisman Trophy is a team award," he said. "If we go into a situation, I don't care who you are—you can be hands-down the most electrifying player in college football and lose two or three games and you're out of that. It's a team award first and foremost because our team is 12–0. I owe them everything in the world. If it wasn't for them in these situations, I wouldn't even be here for any of the accolades that I do receive, and all the credit in the world goes to my team and my coaching staff."

> "I wouldn't even be here for any of the accolades that I do receive, and all the credit in the world goes to my team and my coaching staff."

Defensive lineman David Patterson praised Michigan for giving the Buckeyes all they could handle in an epic battle. So much was at stake for both teams. After laying it all out for 60 minutes, Patterson was overwhelmed. "I can't even explain it, the feeling I'm having right now," Patterson told reporters following the game. "This is the happiest moment of my life. We put in so much hard work with these guys, these young guys, in summer workouts and all the film study, it's just great. It just feels so great when you work really hard for something and everybody's all together. We've been stressing agenda this whole year. The whole agenda—it wasn't just a phrase—we had just one agenda, all the guys, we loved each other and I just thank God, I just thank Jesus."

Ohio State defensive lineman Quinn Pitcock said that the Michigan win went back four years to the 2002 season, when he was a freshman along with fellow freshmen Doug Datish and Patterson. "We learned a lot from the 2002 [national championship] team," Pitcock said. "They had so much heart and character. Throughout the years, we've grown as men through Tressel and his teachings. I think he tries to do that first and foremost, before being a football player. I think that's what the love and the character of our seniors have really brought. And, like David said, just one agenda. We set our mind on what we were going to do and we've done it. And I still can't really believe that we're 12–0."

Tressel praised his seniors for their leadership, loyalty to the program, and focus against a formidable opponent that happened to be their bitterest rival.

"What a special bunch of guys that just worked and worked and led and led," Tressel said. "Everyone told them beginning last spring that we couldn't be a great team because we'd lost so many great players, and these seniors just decided that they were going to do whatever it took to lead a football team to reach its potential. The amount of love that's evident between our players and this senior group is amazing. What I've appreciated about them the most is that they just continue to be humble and just look for ways to get better, and just anything we've ever asked, they've done.

"They've fought like crazy and everything hasn't been perfect, but they haven't given up," Tressel added.

"This is the most fun I've ever had playing a football game in my life," said offensive lineman Doug Datish. "It was just an incredible feeling. I'm just so proud of everybody on the team. This has been the single-most team effort that's gone on through the week of practice on into the game. There were guys, kickers, everybody—those guys weren't standing by the heater vent, they were out there waving the towels around, getting the crowd going. The fans were electric. This was a great atmosphere to root for Ohio State and we were just super excited to get that outright Big Ten title. The guys can look at that sign like I have for five years. They have it for 2006. I'm just super proud of everybody."

Tressel talked about how special the win was for the seniors and how it would be something they will carry with them throughout their lives. "The number one thing in our minds was our seniors and making sure that their last game in this building was a great memory and obviously would lead to the outright Big Ten Championship, which we have not had since 1984," Tressel said. "I guess the sideline of the whole thing is it's going to lead to bigger and better things. But the seniors and the outright Big Ten Championship, that was our focus. Troy mentioned the word focus. Paul Warfield talked to our guys this morning and he talked about those championship teams he was on and they had the ability to concentrate and focus and he really challenged our guys to have that ability amongst all this hoopla and I thought, like they always do, they will listen."

And Tressel made sure to single out the play of Smith at quarterback, and the way he kept his poise and composure, the way Smith remained focused.

"I've said for however many years we've been talking about Troy that his number one quality is his toughness," Tressel said. "If you want to be a champion as a quarterback, toughness is number one. And he is that, and he stands in there and he knows that's part of the game and he pops back up for the next one...."

"I have always enjoyed Troy's passion to be successful," Tressel continued. "From the day I met him, you could tell he had a fire burning inside, that he had some ideas of what he wanted to be, and he has gone on and he has worked hard at that. I really appreciate that. He has always been willing to listen and he is like a sponge for knowledge. I know that's often used, but he really is that."

Smith's perspective? "For me, I live and I play through everybody else. I come back to the huddle, when I stare at 10 guys in the huddle, eyes wide open, alert, and ready to dominate the opposing team, I come to the sideline and there's 105-plus guys, eyes wide open and ready to do everything and anything they can in support of our team. So there's no way that I can get into a situation where I feel as if my legs hurt, my knee is hurt, my elbow is hurt, and limp up or act like something is wrong with my body, because I've been in situations where I've seen scout team players constantly beat their bodies up, play and play and play after play, so I could never shortchange any of my teammates."

Smith's career record against Michigan was astonishing. In three games (and three wins) against the Wolverines, Smith racked up 1,151 yards of total offense, seven passing touchdowns, and two rushing touchdowns. Smith was the first Ohio State quarterback since Tippy Dye (1934–1936) to register three wins against Michigan and the only Buckeyes quarterback to win three straight games against Michigan as a starter.

"I've said it time and time again, it's not me beating Michigan," Smith said, "it's the team that is lined up and took the field every year that I got to start as quarterback that beat Michigan. They're also 3–0. We all have three sets of golden pants and that means the world. You know, that first one, when I first got them, were just a little small, like a Christmas tree ornament, and it didn't mean that much to me at first. But now it means the world because you have to go through situations and games like that today to earn those golden pants and the teams that I've been able to play, we've been privileged to play with, deserve that, just that: to be 3-0."

"I was in the locker room with Troy after the Michigan game," Bob Mansfield recalls. "He came up to me and gave me a big hug and said, 'Everything you said came true.' I said, 'No, everything *Tressel* said came true. I just reiterated it.' Troy became a leader in the locker room and he only became that because of the responsibility, respect, community service, and all those things Troy Smith finally started to believe in, and look what happened."

Although Ohio State ultimately lost to Florida in the national championship game his senior year, Smith acknowledged the magnificent journey he had been on. "During my years at Ohio State, Coach Tressel showed me how much he cared about me as a man first. Football was secondary," Smith said. "Coach Tressel and the coaching staff does a great job of evaluating talent and they know who can play and who can't, but the off-the-field stuff was important to Coach Tressel. He cared about me just as much as Ted Ginn Sr. cared about me. That's how Coach Tressel became a very important part of my life. That's what meant most to me. When we would talk on a personal level, it was always about being a man. It was about your family. Every time we had a break from classes or football and we were going home, he would always tell me and everyone else to make sure to get in contact with your loved ones and see how everybody is doing."

Learning to handle adversity and to overcome odds were things that helped Smith go from a troubled youth to a Heisman trophy winner and an NFL quarterback.

"Nothing in my life has been given to me," he said. "I've had to work for everything. My mind, my body, my spirit, my emotion, and my condition has always been to work hard and strive for everything, that I have to overcome obstacles that have been put in front of me. I wouldn't have it any other way. The people closest to me and the people that know me know who Troy Smith is and what he's going to do. The naysayers are going to be there for the rest of my life and I can't do anything about it. The situations that I encounter come to me for a reason and to a certain extent, I feel like I'm the only one that can handle those situations. And I'll continue to fight through those situations while I'm in the NFL."

14 Trouble in the Program

As much as Tressel tried to run a program devoid of scandal, contro-versy, and infractions, it was an impossible expectation. Troy Smith had his troubles—not once, but twice—but he ultimately rebounded. Of course, there was the Maurice Clarett saga. And there also was Louis Irizarry.

Looking back, he says that if he could have taken back every imma-ture decision, he would—in a heartbeat. But Irizarry, an extremely tal-ented player from Youngstown who had what seemed to be a bright future in football, threw it all away. The immaturity revealed itself when he was recruited in high school. The all-state tight end from Youngstown Ursuline High School first committed to Ohio State while in high school, but not long after, he changed his commitment and opted for the Miami Hurricanes. Then he changed his mind *again*, back to Ohio State.

During Irizarry's first semester at Ohio State, he was involved in a dorm fight. He injured two people and was arrested. He pled guilty to misdemeanor assault and disorderly conduct and was sentenced to three days in jail. He was also suspended from the Buckeyes' foot-ball team for the rest of the season and was placed on probation.

To his credit, he seemed to have moved past that dorm altercation as spring football rolled around. He worked hard during spring prac-tices and solidified himself as a player with potential star quality.

Then came the day that changed Irizarry's life forever. Just days after Ohio State's annual spring game, Irizarry and running back Ira Guilford assaulted and mugged a fellow Ohio State student around

LOUIS IRIZARRY

Position: Tight End

Hometown: Youngstown, Ohio

Years Played: 2003, 2006–2007

Career Highlights: After a promising start at Ohio State, off-the-field indiscretions ended his career as a Buckeye. Irizarry returned to football more focused and mature, and his second act at Youngstown State was impressive.

3:00 AM on the university's campus.

After being arrested, Irizarry and Guilford were brought into a Columbus courtroom in handcuffs to face a judge. Guilford ultimately reached a plea deal in exchange for his testimony against Irizarry.

"I was stupid—really, really stupid—and I had so much remorse for what I had done, and what I put everyone through," Irizarry said. "After I was arrested and was waiting to see what was going to happen to me, my focus changed and I was no longer worried about my homework due Monday or going to practice Saturday morning. As soon as that happened, my focus changed to, *What's going to happen? Am I ever going to go back to college?* I had some pretty bad consequences ahead of me with possible jail time. I really had to learn pretty fast what I would do if all of this fell through and I had to go to jail."

So often, big-time student-athletes feel a sense of entitlement. They can run faster, throw farther, or, in Irizarry's case, catch passes and block better than most players, so they feel they are entitled to the spoils that go along with their exceptional talent. There is a tacit understanding that an athlete can be a jerk off the field, as long as he catches the touchdown pass on the field. To a certain degree, Irizarry had that mentality.

"Before all of this, I don't think I fully understood how good I had it in college," he said. "There was nothing to worry about. I could choose any class. Then, here I was, being classified with a group of people that may not have had the opportunity to go to college or to play in front of 105,000 fans in the Horseshoe.

"I was really down. Really scared. I felt like I blew a once-in-a-million opportunity. I realized that playing football was what I truly loved, because as soon as you don't have something, [you discover] how much you miss it and how much it means to you. I continued to stay in shape even before my court date. I just knew I had to do everything that I could to be ready if the opportunity presented itself for me to play again."

The fact that Irizarry felt remorse was a good sign. In October 2004, he was sentenced to three years in the Correctional Reception Center in Orient, Ohio. The conditions of his sentence stipulated that he had the option after six months to petition for judicial release based on good behavior.

"One of the biggest punishments for me, other than spending time in prison, was that when I got out, I really felt separated from society and didn't feel like I was caught up with the world," Irizarry said.

While in prison, Irizarry made contact with Tressel. It was the first time he had been in contact with his former coach since he was arrested.

"I got a letter back from Coach Tressel not very long after I sent him my letter," Irizarry said. "He said he was glad that I wrote him with my address because he was then able to send me a bunch of

> "He wrote me regularly while I was in there. It was such an uplifting and great feeling."

stuff he wanted to send me, like religious quotes, different inspirational quotes, and things of that nature. He wrote me regularly while I was in there. It was such an uplifting and great feeling. When I would receive letters from Coach Tressel with the Ohio State insignia on the letters, I was filled with pride. It was cool because everybody in prison was impressed that I played for Ohio State and that I knew and played for Coach Tressel."

In one of Tressel's letters to Irizarry, he asked the young man to see him in Columbus when he was released. Tressel wanted to do whatever he could, to the best of his ability, to give Irizarry that second chance. After seven months of serving good time, Irizarry was released from prison in May 2005.

"I came out with this emotional down, like, *Am I worth anything as a person?* Well, the exact day I was released, I went right to Coach Tressel's office in Columbus," Irizarry said. "We talked and he told me he was going to try to get me reinstated at Ohio State and that he would talk to the board of trustees or whoever he had to talk to. And that week he met with them. He got me an answer as soon as he could."

Unfortunately, the answer came back that Irizarry not only wouldn't be permitted to play at Ohio State, but he couldn't play Division I football at all. There was nothing more Tressel could do. "But he was in my corner. That's what meant the most to me," Irizarry said. "That whole summer after my release was just spent looking at colleges and looking at somebody who would take me. I went to every college that had ever spoken to me during high school and no one wanted to give me an opportunity. No one except YSU, and that was even a long shot. People were telling me my career was over and that I would never be able to go back to school. And I didn't know the rules and didn't know if I could. It was a scary and confusing time in my life but I knew in my heart that I didn't want to live with regret and not even try everything in my power to play again."

Tressel spoke to YSU head coach John Heacock about a possible meeting with him and Irizarry. In that meeting, Heacock told Irizarry, "I'm not going to promise you anything. You're going to have to walk on first and start at the bottom."

But Irizarry was a changed person because of his experience. He was a better student and a better worker—and, as a result, a better football player. He entered his senior year ranked as one of the top three tight ends in the Football Championship Subdivision (formerly Division I-AA) by several national scouting services. In his career with the Penguins, he saw action in 21 games, starting nine, and caught 42 passes for 437 yards and three touchdowns. He even received a mini-camp invitation from the Cincinnati Bengals in 2008. SI.com's draft analysis of Irizarry that year was: "(Irizarry) is a naturally gifted prospect with outstanding size/speed numbers. Off-field incidents limited him early in college and an injury kept him on the sidelines as a senior. Presently a free-agent/developmental prospect who possesses a good degree of upside."

"Having gone through everything I went through, all I can say is that I'm grateful that I got another chance to play college football and to go after my dream of playing in the NFL," Irizarry said. "I'm so remorseful because I know I hurt people I didn't know, I hurt my family and it was devastating....

"Something like that won't ever happen again. I was in a constant state of depression, like I was unworthy. But I felt like, as long as I stuck to my plan, an organized plan of what I really wanted to do with my life, it helped me get to where I am now."

Irizarry made big mistakes, mistakes that cost him a potentially outstanding career at Ohio State. With his second chance, he learned from his mistakes and was determined to turn his life around.

Maurice Clarett was a different story altogether. He had the world on a string. As a freshman, he was one of the star players who helped propel the Buckeyes to their 2002 national championship. He looked to be destined for greatness.

Clarett was *USA Today* and *Parade*'s top-ranked high school player at Warren (Ohio) Harding High School, a school that had produced NFL Hall-of-Famer Paul Warfield among a number of other successful college and NFL players. Clarett seemed to have a bright future in Columbus and in the NFL.

His high school coach, Gary Barber, saw Clarett's mental and physical development from a freshman to a senior. He spoke about his first few encounters with Clarett as if were yesterday.

"I remember it vividly," Barber said. "I heard stories about Maurice from middle school. He was an outstanding basketball player, had success in AAU track, and was an incredible football player."

Barber described the first time he saw Clarett on the field. "Right away he caught your attention," Barber said. "It was like watching Herschel Walker at tailback. That's how big and physical and impressive he was, and for him to play at that level at such a young age was absolutely impressive."

Barber also remembered the first day Clarett enrolled at Warren Harding and rolled into the weight room. "He was benching 315 pounds—*as a 15-year old*," Barber recalled in amazement. "We took him to the power lifting championship and he won his weight class as a freshman and was deadlifting 600 pounds. He also was running a 4.5. Those were things that Division I major college running backs were doing at age 21 and 22. But here Maurice was doing those things as a 15-year-old. And he had that work ethic and innate desire that he never wanted to go down as a running back."

Barber said it didn't take very long for him to realize that Clarett had a "very, very keen" idea of where he wanted to be and what he wanted to do with his life. Barber described it as tunnel vision, going through life with blinders on. "Maurice made sure that nothing would distract him along the way," Barber said. "It was almost like an obsessive-compulsive personality with him. If he felt that something wasn't going his way or if he felt that something could distract him, he seemed to replay those things over and over in his mind until he saw things in a different paradigm or [through] a different lens then everyone else."

Barber recalled one year when Warren Harding played conference rival Youngstown Ursuline, a perennial state power in Ohio. Barber was having success getting Clarett the ball on screen passes and other formations in which Clarett lined up wide. So during practice the following week, Barber implemented a few new schemes to featuring Clarett more prominently. "We wanted to get Maurice out in space for several reasons," Barber explained. "For one, he was a heck of a receiver. He was probably one of our best receivers, and he was a running back. Second, not a lot of defensive backs could tackle him in the open field. And lastly, it enabled us to diversify our offense using him in different sets like that."

But Clarett was aggravated with the new formations. "The next day at practice, Maurice had a conversation with our running backs coach about our game plan that wasn't very positive at all," Barber said. "As a coaching staff, we had to sit him down and explain to him that we were doing this because he was such a dynamic and versatile player for us and we just wanted to use him even more.

"In my opinion, I think he thought about it and thought about it and played it over and over in his mind and convinced himself that we were trying to move him from running back and make him into a wide receiver," Barber said.

Clarett's first game as a varsity player at Warren Harding was spectacular. Yet, Barber said Clarett was never fully healthy in high school. The Raiders opened with Cleveland Benedictine, which was coming off a state championship season. Clarett carried the ball 17 times for 117 yards and five touchdowns. He went on to have an outstanding freshman season despite battling an ankle injury. That's when the college recruiting circus and the "Maurice Clarett sweepstakes" began.

Barber said Clarett's football IQ was impressive. "I remember taking Maurice to Michigan for a spring practice," Barber said. "Most kids his age wanted to see the weight room and tour the stadium. Maurice wanted to sit in on the running back's meeting to see what was going on and how they did things.

"Our coaches would take some of the older players to campuses for visits. A group of players were going to the University of Indiana and Maurice wanted to go to see the facilities. Maurice was so impressed that when he came home, he committed to Indiana. So I had a conversation with him and said, 'Maurice, this is four years away. Things change. You don't need to make a commitment like this.'

"A few months later, he committed to Notre Dame. Again, he was young and getting all that [mail] and attention because everybody knew about him."

Clarett's ankle injury followed him into his sophomore season. But even playing on reduced time because of injury, Clarett still rushed for more than 1,000 yards. "His junior year, he still had that injury to deal with," Barber said. "He eventually had to sit out the first half of his senior year. He was really never healthy for us."

Despite his injury, he was still a hot prospect, ultimately settling on Ohio State as his choice for college ball. Clarett's first and only season at OSU was remarkable. He rushed for 1,237 yards, a school record for a freshman, and scored 18 touchdowns. His five-yard touchdown run was the game-winner for the Buckeyes in the second overtime of their 31–24 win against the Miami Hurricanes in the 2003 Fiesta Bowl, securing a national championship. Clarett was the first freshman to be the leading rusher on a national championship team since Georgia running back and Heisman winner Herschel Walker did it in 1980.

During the Fiesta Bowl press conference, then–Miami head coach Larry Coker was asked if he could compare his star running back, Willis McGahee, to an NFL player. Coker obliged by offering up Hall-of-Famer Barry Sanders. Tressel was asked the same question about Clarett. He couldn't draw comparisons.

"I don't think I've ever coached anyone exactly like Maurice Clarett that you would be aware of," he said. "I had a young guy from Youngstown that has two or three championship rings that would probably be the first guy that would pop up in my mind that was like him." (He may have been referring to Youngstown State running back Tamron Smith, who played in three national championships from 1991 through 1993 and won two.)

After helping Ohio State win the 2002 national championship, the trouble started. Clarett was suspended from the team during the 2003 season after it was revealed that he filed a false police report in January of 2003 claiming that he had $10,000 worth of merchandise stolen from a car he was using. Clarett never returned to the team after the suspension.

He later challenged the National Football League's rules on under-classmen entering the draft, and lost. He decided that he would forgo the rest of his collegiate career and head straight to the NFL. The Denver Broncos surprisingly took a chance on Clarett, drafting him in the third round of the 2005 NFL draft in April. Broncos coach Mike Shanahan, a well-respected man in NFL circles, thought Clarett still had a future. But before the season even started, Clarett was cut. Shanahan later admitted he made a big mistake.

"When I heard Mike Shanahan say Maurice is not a good team-mate, doesn't have a good work ethic, and doesn't know how to practice, [coming] from someone like Mike Shanahan, who is pretty much one of the most well-respected coaches in the NFL...it pretty much put a black mark on Maurice in the NFL for the rest of his life," Barber said. "I hear something like that, and that's not the way I ever remembered him. To hear that Maurice's work ethic changed was the only thing that was puzzling to me."

In January of 2006, Clarett was arrested and charged with aggra-vated robbery after revealing a handgun to a couple in the alley outside a Columbus nightclub and stealing one of the victims' cell phones.

Later that year, he was arrested once again in Columbus for hav-ing four semi-automatic rifles, a handgun, and a half bottle of Grey Goose vodka all on the passenger seat of his car. He was wearing a bulletproof vest. Reports said Clarett was pulled over for a traffic violation and a struggle ensued. Police had to use tear gas on Clarett because his bulletproof vest rendered the tasers ineffective. He was stopped a few blocks away from the home of a witness who was scheduled to testify against him in the robbery case. Rumor had it that Clarett planned to intimidate the witness by shooting up his house.

How could a young man with such amazing talent and potential lose it all? Barber reflected, "Am I surprised at how things turned out for him? Absolutely. The fact that he had all of these legal issues surprised and saddened me.... In the time he spent with my wife and our family, he definitely made a big impression on them because he was such a very, very kind and appreciative person. And that smile he would have on his face all the time would just light up a room. It's just so sad the way his story turned out....

"Do all kids learn from their mistakes? You hope."

[Author's note: I had written about the Clarett affair in a 2006 column for the *Akron Beacon Journal*.]

I was visiting my wife's family in Youngstown and happened to catch the local 6 o'clock news. The sports segment came on and the anchor led with a story that I just couldn't believe. It was about Maurice Clarett. As I watched, I couldn't help but think, *David Letterman couldn't have written a better joke.*

This probably would have been his delivery:

"Folks, you remember former Ohio State running back and Heisman hopeful Maurice Clarett. Well, the young man was indicted in February on two counts of aggravated robbery. He allegedly tried to rob two people with a .45 caliber handgun on January 1 in Columbus. If he's convicted, he could be sentenced up to 25 years in prison.

"In the meantime, Clarett is keeping his hopes of playing in the pros alive. He held a press conference Thursday to announce he's playing for an indoor professional football team called the Mahoning Valley Hitmen. That's right folks, the *Hitmen*."

Cue Paul Shaffer doubling over in laughter.

Unfortunately, the team neverplayed a game as the organization never materialized past Clarett's press conference.

Don't get me wrong, I'm not making light of Clarett's legal situation. But his was a very auspicious end to a promising career.

As a freshman in college, Clarett had the world in the palm of his hand. After winning the national championship, he was frequently seen at St. Vincent–St. Mary basketball games, giving the media the impression that Clarett and LeBron James were best friends. Not so; they were young stars on the rise who happened to be from the same area. But the story lines associated with the two athletes illustrated the perils and rewards that come with handling meteoric success at a young age.

Behind closed doors and speaking about Clarett's demise, Tressel said, "Maurice is a troubled young man. Let's just pray for him."

Not all of the Buckeyes' biggest struggles were with their players and the law. The loss to Florida in the 2006 national championship was a particularly low point.

"Everyone will tell you, that Florida loss in the national championship game was a wake-up call," Bob Mansfield said. "Coach Tressel interviewed everybody on that team individually for about 45 minutes or close to an hour and asked where the breakdowns were. In my opinion, I think the breakdown came in the form of a little bit of complacency. You get spoiled somewhat when you're 12–0 and you get the kind of hype we got from the media after beating Michigan. Now, you're asking these guys to get prepared for a national championship game where, in many of their minds, they felt they had just won the national championship [by beating] Michigan, which was ranked No. 2 in the country, and we were ranked No. 1.

"In the national championship game, I didn't think our guys played with an attitude. They didn't play to win, they played not to lose."

MIKE KUDLA

Position: Linebacker

Hometown: Medina, Ohio

Years Played: 2002–2005

Career Highlights: Kudla was one of the strongest players to ever play at Ohio State. He set a team record with his 610-pound bench press and was the team's Most Valuable Defensive Player in 2005.

Then came the bad news about linebacker Mike Kudla. Kudla was probably one of the strongest defensive players to ever don a Buckeyes' uniform. He set the team record with a 610-pound bench press, obliterating his old record of 555 pounds.

His health problems started right after the 2002 national championship game. The team flew back from Tempe, Arizona, and on the Thursday after the Tuesday win, Kudla became really sick. By Saturday, he was put into the infectious disease ward at the Ohio State University Hospital. From there, Kudla recalled, it was touch-and-go. He was diagnosed with Stevens-Johnson Syndrome, a life-threatening disease that severely affected his immune system.

"I ended up having eight fatal infectious diseases at one point and miraculously I was able to pull through it," Kudla said. "My immune system [was] so suppressed from mono that it became obsolete and it could no longer continue to fight off anything. My immune system just basically shut down. Luckily, I had the body size and mass that I was able to lose the body weight. I ended up losing 52 pounds and went through a rash of infections....

"The good thing about the ordeal [was] having coaches like Coach Tressel and the rest of the staff...always there with me. They would call in, and the doctors or my mom would hold the phone up for me. If they didn't call, they sent cards; the whole team did. They all would always make sure to touch base with me. It made me feel like I was still part of the football family.

"After I got healthy, I realized that things could have been much worse for me," Kudla said. "Disease, illness, and people off at war really brings your own life into perspective."

Tressel didn't let Kudla feel sorry for himself. Instead, he helped Kudla understand that the fact that he was healthy and alive meant more than any championship trophy or any dollar amount that anyone could put on a professional football salary.

"We all loved Mike and his family, so we told him to just concentrate and focus on the little things because that's the most important thing in life: your family and friends," Tressel said. "That was the big picture for Mike."

Kudla fought through his illness and signed a free agent contract with the Pittsburgh Steelers after his senior year. He was released, but signed a free agent contract with the Cleveland Browns in 2007. Those trying times helped shaped Kudla as a man. It also helped shape his lasting friendship with Tressel, long after Kudla's collegiate and professional days were over.

"When Coach Tressel recruited me, he knew my mom and dad and brothers and sisters by name," Kudla said. "He continued that relationship with me and my family throughout my college years and he continues that relationship now in my professional career. He doesn't look at me any differently than he did on the first day I met him. That's why I love him."

RAY ISAAC

Position: Quarterback

Hometown: Youngstown, Ohio

Years Played: 1988–1991

Career Highlights: Isaac guided the Penguins to their first-ever Division I-AA national championship in 1991 and was named the team MVP. He is second on the school's leaderboards for rushing yards by a quarterback (1,341) and touchdowns by a quarterback (23).

The love that former Youngstown State quarterback Ray Isaac had for Tressel was special. Isaac, who was nicknamed "the Colonel" because of his leadership abilities, was Tressel's first national championship quarterback.

He was home-grown, a product of the Rayen School in Youngstown, who stayed home to play for Tressel. He is arguably one of Youngstown State's all-time gifted athletes. Tressel has a fondness for Isaac not just because Isaac was a quarterback, like Tressel was, but also because he is a carefree, personable, likable young man.

When Isaac was on the football field, he was routinely one of the best athletes on the field, regardless of the competition. Off the field, however, he was the focus of an NCAA investigation that alleged he had accepted close to $10,000 in money and gifts.

Isaac was convicted of a felony and served time because of his improper actions while an athlete at YSU. "I tell you what, being a convicted felon and pleading guilty to a fel-ony is a long road. I'm still on a tedious road," Isaac said.

After his release, he returned to the game to play arena football. He acknowledges, "I didn't have [anything] but football, so I tried to go out and get hooked up with the teams I could. Any teams, any-where. Chasing that dream cost me my family."

Isaac's illegal actions also cost him his collegiate family. People like Tressel and Isaac's teammates and friends never abandoned him, and the university tried its best to support Isaac, but they could only do so much. He could not continue his education or his football career at YSU.

"I love Youngstown State University," Isaac said, with conviction. "They don't know how bad it hurts not being inducted into the Collegiate Hall of Fame or how bad it hurts not being invited to football games. I know I made mistakes, but I put my heart and soul into that university. Still, you can't take my national championship away from me. You can't take my undefeated season. You can't take away that I was the first quarterback in YSU history to make it to the national championship. You can't take those things away from me."

15 "Pryor" Knowledge of the 2008 Season

The Terrelle Pryor sweepstakes were high. The highly touted 6'6", 230-pound quarterback out of Jeannette, Pennsylvania, could have picked any school in the country. Conventional wisdom had him staying in his home state and playing for the legendary Joe Paterno at Penn State. There was also talk that Pryor would go to Michigan to play for first-year coach Rick Rodriguez, who was heavily recruiting Pryor from his previous post at West Virginia. Naturally, Tressel and Ohio State were in the recruiting mix, too. When the official national letter of intent day rolled around, Pryor held a press conference at his high school to finally announce his choice.

The announcement was more of a non-announcement: he hadn't decided. It took six more weeks and several more college visits, but in the end, he chose Ohio State.

What Pryor accomplished in his high school career was astonishing. The two-time Pennsylvania Player of the Year led his high school to back-to-back state championships and was the first Pennsylvania player to pass and rush for more than 4,000 yards. He also scored a school-record 2,285 career points and helped his school win the state basketball championship his senior year as well.

But Pryor's high school accomplishments were just that: high school accomplishments. He still had to prove that he could translate those skills to the collegiate level. He was also not automatically handed the job. The Buckeyes already had a well-established quarterback in senior Todd Boeckman, an outstanding leader and the team captain for Ohio State in his junior year. Boeckman led the Buckeyes to an

11–2 record and a trip to the BCS National Championship game. He finished the season passing for 2,379 yards and 25 touchdowns and was named the Big Ten Offensive Player of the Year.

There was no talk whatsoever about Pryor sharing snaps with Boeckman at all. And Tressel's history as a head coach dictated that. The coach always rewarded loyalty and he was consistent in bringing along his young quarterbacks until he felt they were ready and equipped with the mental and physical skills needed to be his leader.

But Ohio State's soft schedule in the first few weeks of the season gave Tressel a chance to put Pryor in for a few snaps and to bank some experience. Pryor's first game was in the season-opener in the Horseshoe against Youngstown State. The Buckeyes, ranked No. 2 in the country, won 43–0.

Pryor made his official debut with 6:52 left in the first quarter and the Buckeyes leading 10–0. In his first snap, he dropped back and completed a nine-yard pass to Lamaar Thomas. Pryor eventually led Ohio State on a 12-play, 51-yard scoring drive that gave the Buckeyes a 13-0 lead thanks to a 31-yard field goal by Ryan Pretorius.

In his first collegiate game, Pryor was 4-of-6 for 35 yards. He scored his first touchdown as a Buckeye on an 18-yard run early in the fourth quarter and also had a nice 21-yard run in the fourth quarter. Ohio State fans had a glimpse of what the future held for the quarterback.

Pryor's future at Ohio State took center stage sooner than most thought, especially Tressel. Ohio State headed into the much-hyped USC game on September 13 at the Rose Bowl in Los Angeles ranked No. 5, but with dubious wins against Youngstown State and Ohio University. Ohio State was winning, but they were struggling. And the loss of key running back Beanie Wells only fueled the skeptics' fires. Meanwhile, No. 1-ranked USC, led by quarterback Mark Sanchez, was rolling over opponents.

Boeckman started against USC and Ohio State's best series of the game was its second: a 17-play, 69-yard scoring drive. But the

Buckeyes had to settle for a 29-yard Pretorius field goal for a 3–0 lead. It was disheartening for Ohio State to drive all the way down the field, only to come up with a field goal.

It was all downhill from there as the Trojans dominated the rest of the contest to cast further doubt on Ohio State. But at the same time, it ushered in the Terrelle Pryor era. The freshman was named the starter for the next week, and never relinquished the position again.

It was the first time a true freshman started at quarterback for Ohio State since Art Schlichter started for the Buckeyes in 1978. In Pryor's first career start, he went 10-of-16 for 139 yards and four touchdowns (a record for a freshman passer).

In postgame interviews, he was modest about his performance.

"I thought I messed up a lot," Pryor said. "When we sit down in the film room, I'm going to get yelled at, but that's a good thing."

When asked about his record-setting day, he remained humble. "That goes with the wide receivers and offensive linemen," he said. "Without both of them, it wouldn't happen. It's as much their record as it is mine."

And Pryor sounded almost embarrassed to answer questions about replacing Boeckman as the starter. He had ample respect for the senior captain. "Todd is a great quarterback," Pryor said proudly of his teammate. "I looked up to him before I got here. Starting my freshman year never even crossed my mind when I committed, so it came as a big surprise."

Those who knew Tressel well, like former Youngstown State quarterback Mark Brungard, also were surprised that Pryor took over Boeckman's job.

"When Coach Tressel went with Pryor full time, I have to admit it did surprise me because that's something that I don't think Coach Tressel has ever done—especially with a leader like Boeckman," Brungard said. "That told you that Pryor was special."

Former Ohio State quarterback Justin Zwick could relate. "There was a lot of excitement with Terrelle coming in, which was deserved because he was a great [high school] player," he said. "I think just the way things happened throughout the season, like the USC loss and the way the Trojans got pressure on Boeckman in that game, I think it was just in Coach Tressel's mind that it was better to...get a guy back there who can run around a little bit, and Terrelle did that.

"But Todd...did an exceptional job handling himself through all of that. He was a great mentor for Terrelle, and I knew that from talking to Todd. He was always supportive of Terrelle and you can't say enough about Todd. He was still the team leader and the ultimate team player and played the captain role to a 'T' in going through what he did.... He needed to help his team and stay positive, and he knew he needed to help Terrelle because he...was young and was going to need it."

Pryor had a standout first season, and led the Buckeyes in a veritable drubbing of archrival Michigan on November 22. But one of the most emotional moments of the lopsided game came early in the fourth quarter when Boeckman—the player who had been the leader of the offense for the past two seasons, the player who was voted the offensive MVP of the Big Ten the previous year, the player who was rock-steady all during the 2007 season in leading the Buckeyes to the national championship game against LSU—entered the game at Ohio Stadium that day for the first and very last time.

The crowd rose to its feet and cheered with passion for Boeckman. They wanted to show the classy young man that they appreciated everything that he did for the program, as his career was coming to a close. They cheered for accomplishments, but moreover for his class and character. It was in these characteristics that Tressel's stamp was indelible.

16 Bowl Busts

Before Ohio State matched up with the Florida in the 2007 national championship game, Ohio State quarterback Troy Smith said it was going to be a "scary" situation, but not because he feared the Gators' defense.

"It is going to be very emotional for me because this is the last time this group of guys will be together," Smith said. "And I think it is scary. I think it is scary for two reasons. One, because you are not promised tomorrow. Who is to say what's going to happen as soon as you leave here? And, two, I love every single one of my teammates and I won't be able to sit down in the locker room and sit next to Anthony Gonzalez again. I won't be able to go onto the field and crack jokes with Antonio Pittman. I won't be able to slap high fives wearing the Ohio State colors with Doug Datish again."

Reporters tried hyping the game like a pay-per-view boxing event, trying to coax both head coaches—Tressel and Florida coach Urban Meyer—into saying something. When asked why he thought Ohio State was going to win, Tressel wouldn't bite.

"I don't know if I have ever said that I believe we are going to win," he said. "I believe that we've got good kids. I believe that we have guys that have worked hard to understand in this matchup, what it is going to take to be successful. I believe in our kids.

"But I think you play the game one day at a time in preparation, and one play at a time. If you start thinking about and predicting what the outcome is going to be, I think you have lost sight of the task at hand."

A reporter tried asking the same question, but in a different way. "Do you think you are better than the Gators?" the reporter asked.

"I believe we are a good football team. We haven't played the Gators. I think they're outstanding. I have watched them on film: great preparation, great speed, excellent creativity. I think that's why we are having the game," he countered

Then, the game began and, in all reality, ended on one play. On the opening kickoff, the Ohio State wide receiver and kick returner Ted Ginn Jr. pulled in the kick and left the entire Florida kickoff team in the dust, blazing all the way down the field for a touchdown.

Unfortunately, that was the end for Ginn and the Buckeyes. During celebrations in the end zone, Ginn suffered an ankle injury that took him out of the game. Everything went downhill for Ohio State after that as the Buckeyes were completely outplayed, losing to Florida 41–14.

It was later revealed that Ginn broke his ankle during the end zone celebration. Ted Ginn Sr. said his son's injury devastated Tressel on a personal level because the two were so close. "Had Ted not come out of a program like Ohio State and had his experience with Coach Tressel, Ted would have struggled even more with the foot injury," Ginn Sr. said.

"The first thing Coach Tressel said to me after the Florida game was, 'Coach Ginn, I had all my Teddy plays ready. Had them all ready.' Coach Tressel was really disappointed and hurt for Ted and I could see it in his face and hear it in his voice. I think Coach Tressel felt really bad Ted's [college] career ended that way. It's just my own personal feeling but I think it's something that bothered Coach Tressel for a while because he really wanted Ted to end his career in a positive way. I've heard Coach Tressel say that some people are made to be just good people, and that's something he said about my son and I'll always remember that."

At the same time, Tressel knew that in this game, injuries happen and one player doesn't make the difference. "Well, you know, I think sometimes when you lose a guy that's a big part of what you do and constantly gave you sparks throughout the course of the years…it affects you," Tressel said. "But, again, that's part of the game. And you have to create the depth. You have to create the broad approach so that you know if you lose a guy here or there you're going to survive. But it certainly didn't help."

Troy Smith echoed his coach.

"I've never been a believer [that] things like that can take us out of a game. Don't get me wrong, he's a great player, sensational player, a phenomenal player—on and off the field. When we're on the sideline, he gives us a boost…. And not having him in spirits definitely took a little bit away from the team."

Reflecting on the game, Smith said he had no regrets. "We came out, we fought. If we come up short and…this is the worst thing that happens in life to us, then I'm pretty cool. But, you know, the other guys, my seniors, I want to apologize to them because I wasn't able to send them out on the right note."

"I think we at times put Troy in a situation that was tough," Tressel jumped in. "And [we] didn't give ourselves as good a chance as we could…. I appreciate Troy's willingness to burden a lot, but he's burdened a lot this whole year. And I have to say, it was a combined effort, starting with the coaches."

"I'm a firm believer in 'what happens to you is meant to happen,'" Smith said. "There are so many other things that makes these seniors smile," he said, proudly. "And I know this year made so many people happy in the state of Ohio. You're not going to be able to…have a storybook ending all the time.

"In this kind of situation, I'm a realist," Smith continued, as if he were delivering a spiritual sermon. "I have an understanding that not everything in life is going to go the exact same way that you want it to."

It was clear that the coach had left an impression on his young quarterback. Smith's attitude and philosophy closely resembled his coach's.

Wide receiver Roy Hall looked at the loss as a source of motivation for the team in its next season. "After losing the national championship to Florida like we did, I learned that life will keep dealing you blows no matter how hard you work. If you want to be successful, you're going to have to get knocked down so that you can work even harder the next time to get that success," Hall said. "For the guys coming back, it will show whether or not that Florida game affected their hunger. If they go out in the first couple of games and barely win then get a couple losses, people might say they were still feeling that Florida loss. If they bounce back and they are successful, people will say they are ready to fight. You just have to take advantage of every opportunity because it may take them three or four years or maybe even longer to get back to the national championship game."

Hall's statement proved prophetic, as Ohio State took care of business, winning their first 10 games. A late season slip against Illinois had them tumbling down the polls, but with a little help from other teams, they found themselves back in the BCS national championship game—this time against another SEC team, LSU, and at the Superdome in New Orleans, ostensibly LSU's own backyard.

During press conferences leading up to the game, offensive tackle Kirk Barton, who was known for his colorful comments throughout his collegiate career at Ohio State, reflected on how and why the Buckeyes made it back to the title game.

"Compared to last season, you know it's just kind of a different mentality.... A lot of people doubted us going into the season....

"We don't really care what the pundits and critics [say].... We were able to believe in each other, and our staff believed in us. And we were able to get back to where we wanted to be."

With all the hype, interviews, and pre-game prognostications behind them, the clash between Ohio State and LSU commenced. And once again, it was Ohio State striking quick as Beanie Wells put the Buckeyes ahead 7–0 just four plays into the game on a 65-yard run. Ohio State's defense forced the Tigers to punt on their first possession of the game and the Buckeyes' offense went right back to work. Ryan Pretorius tacked on a 25-yard field goal a few minutes later and Ohio State went ahead 10-0.

They looked like a totally different Ohio State team than the one that showed up against Florida in the national championship a year earlier. Unfortunately, LSU scored 31 unanswered points and rolled to a 38–24 victory. It was another heartbreak for the team that had seen its share. But the chance for redemption is always on the road ahead.

17 Looking for Redemption and Respect in Arizona

On the day of the 2009 Tostito Fiesta Bowl between Ohio State and Texas, Ohio State graduate and Youngstown native and attorney Lou Schiavoni was one happy man. He was sitting in the Statehouse in Columbus with his family and friends to watch his son, 29-year-old Joe—who was also an attorney and worked with his father in Youngstown at their firm of Schiavoni, Schiavoni, Muldowney, & Bush, take the oath as a state senator. An Ohio State graduate and longtime season-ticket holder, the elder Schiavoni had been hyped up about the Fiesta Bowl since it was announced. So were his four sons. He couldn't help but think about that big game. Senator Schiavoni had to be thinking the same thing, even if he wouldn't admit it.

After being dismantled in two consecutive BCS national championship games by SEC teams, no one gave Ohio State a snowball's chance in the 2009 Tostitos Fiesta Bowl against the heavily favored, high-powered Texas offense led by junior quarterback Colt McCoy. And the reality was that the Buckeyes had lost a lot of respect because of their past two losses.

Kirk Herbstreit, a former Ohio State quarterback who went on to be one of the top college football analysts in the country with ESPN and ABC, was known for being an outspoken critic of his alma mater when it was warranted. But it was his job to be objective. Prior to the Ohio State–Texas matchup, Herbstreit was spot-on with his analysis: "[With] everything that's happened to them on the big stage, it's a chance for them to gain back some credibility."

The Buckeyes fell 16 seconds short of notching a huge win. It was another heartbreak for Ohio State.

But with Pryor showing so much potential in just his first year, there was a lot Ohio State fans could look forward to in the years to come. Texas coach Mack Brown said Pryor reminded him of his former outstanding quarterback, Vince Young, who was the 2005 Heisman runner-up.

"Terrelle Pryor played an unbelievable game, the best I have seen him. And I think that's a preview of what we will see in him for the future," Brown said after the game. "There is no doubt, at some point he has a chance to lead them to a national championship. He will be a guy that's in a Heisman race and it may be sooner than we think because he is a leader."

Tressel, looking at what his seniors accomplished over their careers, wanted people to look at their body of work.

"I can't tell you how proud I am of the leadership of guys like James [Laurinitis] and Brian [Rubiskie] and those other seniors," Tressel said. "We wanted so badly to send them out in a big way, and we didn't get that done on the scoreboard, but I think they know by how hard their teammates played and prepared and how much we all care about them.

"As I said at the outset, I'm so proud of the leadership these guys had, the character they have, what they do on and off the field. Most importantly, who they are. They are first-class people and great ambassadors for college football and for Ohio State. And we are going to miss them very, very, very much."

It was a bittersweet end for the outgoing seniors, but they were rightly reminded that they take with them much more than just the outcome of their last game.

18 The Coach's Coach

In 2007, the Indianapolis Colts, defending Super Bowl Champs, chose four Ohio State players through the draft and free agency.

"I definitely don't think it's a coincidence that the Indianapolis Colts had four former Ohio State players on the roster, including myself, Anthony Gonzalez, Quinn Pitcock, and Antonio Smith," former Ohio State wide receiver Roy Hall said. "Players are drafted off of many things. Sometimes it's potential, but mostly it's talent. But then you have a situation where you have two guys that are equal across the board but one has character issues. I feel [Colts head coach] Tony Dungy and Coach Tressel have a similar system in what they look for as far as class and character and who they want playing within their program.

"We're all guys who will come in and work hard. Every once in a while, all of us former Buckeyes will wear this T-shirt that has a saying by Woody Hayes that says, 'You win with people,'" Hall said. "That's the truth, and at the end of the day, it comes down to the people that are going to work hard together and the people who aren't going to give you any problems and I think that's why we all ended up in Indianapolis."

Dungy is also a coach's coach. His Colts players, including All-Pro and Super Bowl MVP quarterback Peyton Manning, feel privileged to play for a man of great character and integrity. Dungy has expressed similar things about Tressel.

"Jim is a great football coach who has taken two programs to championship heights," Dungy said. "But what I admire about him, though, is *how* he has done it. Coach Tressel is a man of integrity and that comes across in how his teams play and the type of young men he develops. He teaches them not only how to play the game, but helps them grow as men and as role models. I have a 15-year-old son and I would love it if he would have the opportunity to play for Jim Tressel because I know he would come away a better person."

> "Tressel is a man of integrity and that comes across in how his teams play and the type of young men he develops. He teaches them not only how to play the game, but helps them grow as men and as role models."

Mark Dantonio, who took over as head coach at Michigan State in 2007, was on Tressel's inaugural staff at Youngstown State in 1986, then coached with Tressel at Ohio State and later made a name for himself as a head coach. He was hired in 2003 to be the head coach at Cincinnati, where he coached three seasons and became the first head coach in 23 years to lead the school to a winning season in his first season. Dantonio was named the head coach at Michigan State in November of 2006.

One of the first things that Dantonio did when he got the job at Cincinnati was to mirror his program after what Tressel had established at Youngstown State and Ohio State. Every one of Tressel's former assistant coaches took that approach with them to head coaching jobs. "When I was first at Michigan State, I went back to Youngstown State to speak at a clinic," Dantonio said. "Coach Tressel also was there and I remember talking to him in the parking lot afterward and asked him how he's been able to be so successful. I think his secret is that he's been able to harness the human spirit. I really do. That's based on him incorporating all of the things he teaches the players, instead of just the football player, building all the things that really make the difference in a person."

Coaches are always learning from other coaches, borrowing each other's philosophies and concepts, then adding their innovations. It

Longtime Cleveland Glenville Coach and father of former Ohio State star wide receiver Ted Ginn Jr., Ted Ginn Sr. commands his players' attention prior to a game.

is a fraternity that is centered around respect. Tressel has respect for all coaches, and grew up as a coach's son. The relationship Tressel had with coach Ted Ginn Sr. was also very influential.

"Coach Ginn and his staff have done a terrific job since he took over the program there," Tressel said. "When he took over and really put his signature on how he helps kids grow, their program took off. He has been very fortunate to have outstanding athletes. I don't know the exact number of Division I football players he's had, but there was one point in time when his high school had the fourth-most Division I guys...

"There are a lot of college teams around the country that have gotten better because they have had his kids, and we certainly have been fortunate because our [Glenville] kids have done a great job," Tressel said.

Ginn Sr. was a strong-minded disciplinarian at one of Cleveland's urban schools. In the fall of 2007, he opened Ginn Academy, an all-boys boarding school in the inner city that houses, educates, and mentors young boys who are at risk. "I've never won the state title in football in all the years I've been coaching, and I really don't care if I do," Ginn Sr. said. "When you win kids' hearts, minds, and souls, it means more than anything in the world. What I've realized over the years in dealing with children is that they are going to break your heart. But I've had more kids that made my heart feel warm than [those] breaking it. But when a kid breaks my heart by not following those instructions that you gave them or by not following the rules, the core values of life, then I feel like I've failed the kid.

"I've had kids who get into trouble and don't finish college and that bugs me," Ginn Sr. said. "But when you get a kid to come back and say 'I wouldn't be who I am and where I am if Coach Tressel or Coach Ginn hadn't taught me the core values of life,' that's what means the most to me."

Ginn was known for making all of his student-athletes accountable for their actions on and off the field. He always wanted more out of his athletes, sometimes wanting more from the players than they wanted and demanded out of themselves. It was the love Ginn Sr. had for his student-athletes that made him want them to reach their full potential and feel that anything short of that was unacceptable.

Tressel is like that in so many ways. No matter how fast a player can run or how far he can throw the ball or how much he can lift, Tressel wants to his players to reach their full potential. Ginn appreciated the fact that Tressel wanted Ginn's son, Ted Ginn Jr., to reach his full potential on the football field.

"When Coach Tressel decided he wanted to move Ted from cornerback to wide receiver, that was something that I hadn't thought about prior to Coach Tressel bringing it up," Ginn Sr. said. Ted Jr. was named the Defensive Player of the Year by *USA Today* in his senior year of high school. "Coach Tressel called me from a coach's standpoint and a father's standpoint and wanted my opinion. And that move changed Ted's career. It made Ted more valuable in college and it made him more valuable going to the next level. He wasn't a one-dimensional player anymore because you take a kid like Ted and he can play receiver, punt, kickoff return, and cornerback. Coach Tressel deciding to do that, and having the respect for me as a father and a coach to ask my opinion about his idea meant a lot to me."

That move eventually helped Ginn Jr. become an All-American wide receiver at Ohio State and one of the most feared kick return specialists in the country. He also ended up being the No. 9 pick in the 2007 NFL draft. Some experts said Ginn Jr. could have gone higher in the draft but a foot injury on the opening kickoff of the 2006 national championship game against Florida—which he returned for a touchdown—was a concern. After that touchdown, Ginn Jr. didn't play the rest of the game.

When you can make an impact on a former NFL owner whose team won five Super Bowls, it means something. Tressel and former San Francisco 49ers owner Eddie J. DeBartolo Jr., a billionaire and Youngstown native, have been friends for years. DeBartolo was owner of the 49ers during its heydays with Joe Montana, Jerry Rice, Ronnie Lott, Steve Young, and the late head coach Bill Walsh. DeBartolo was always fascinated with Tressel's approach to the game and to life.

"Jim is such a tactician," DeBartolo said. "He's a brilliant coach. I think the biggest thing that makes him so unique as a coach is that he relates well and knows how to handle his players. That's something you look for in the business world. Jim has a knack for that, which I actually saw in Bill Walsh when I hired him as our head coach. They both go for players who are smart and basically fit into their scheme and their coaching ability. It's really easy to say a guy is a great coach after he's been successful and after he's won Super Bowls or NCAA national championships. Those coaches aren't made, they are born. And I really think Jim was born to be a great coach.

"As far as the similarities I see in Bill and Jim, well, they both are steady. Nothing seems to fluster them," DeBartolo said. "They have a program and they have a plan. They don't [deviate] from their plan. If they have some bad things happen, things they can't control, they don't vary from the way they operate."

Several of Tressel's former players have gone on to become coaches themselves. Joe Nohra credits most of his success to Tressel and his advice and philosophies about life during Nohra's time at YSU, though that time was cut short because of injuries.

He played for three years and then told Tressel that he was leaving the team because he wasn't playing and couldn't play well any longer as a result of his injury. "I told Coach Tressel that he should give my scholarship to someone more deserving," Nohra said. Tressel wasn't going to let Nohra off the hook easily. "Coach Tressel said, 'Joe. Go back and think of your role right now. You're role isn't a starter; you're not a starter. But by practicing and being on the scout team, you're role is just as important as a starter—your job is to make the starters better.'" Tressel told Nohra to keep his scholarship and if he didn't think his role as a player on the team was good enough, he could quit playing, keep the scholarship, and remain on the team as a student coach. Instead, Nohra flat-out quit the team.

"Coach Tressel desperately tried to get me to do the right thing, but unfortunately, I didn't learn about it until later in life when I became a coach at St. Thomas Aquinas [in Louisville, Ohio]," Nohra said. "That's one of my biggest regrets, that I didn't learn that at the time he was trying to teach it to me, and I left the team anyway. I didn't make correct decisions with what was going on in my life at the time but Coach Tressel made every effort he could to teach me the right way to do things.

There wasn't a time during his coaching career at Youngstown State or Ohio State that Tressel didn't give his players the "thumbs up" when they needed some encouragement or inspiration.

"Now, I've gone on and used that story to help motivate the players that I've coached," Nohra said. "I tell every kid that I've ever coached that they have a role. Even the senior that's not starting, you have a role and you can't stop and look back. You have to work hard and move forward for the betterment of the team, the family. I took that same model Coach Tressel had and used it in my coaching philosophy. I always met individually with my players during the preseason, during the season, and in the off-season."

One year, he had a situation with one of his players that was exactly like his own situation at YSU. "I was the head coach and I had a senior that I felt I needed to get on the field," Nohra said. "So at a junior varsity game on a Saturday, I brought him in and said, 'Look son, you're not playing varsity and I need in my heart for you to play some football besides practice.' I gave the *same* speech to him that Coach Tressel gave to me. The kid wasn't happy at the time, but I told him his role as a senior was to get the rest of the team ready by pushing them. I wanted to reward him with playing time in the junior varsity game. Afterward, his father was livid with me. But I had to be honest with people and you can't sugarcoat things. If they are not good enough to play, you tell them. But you tell them to keep working hard so that they give themselves a chance to improve and possibly earn more playing time. I feel that I've been a successful head coach because of my experience with Coach Tressel."

Nohra recalls another time when Tressel suspected Nohra was distracted by something going on in his life. Nohra said Tressel had a keen sense of knowing when something was bothering one of his players. For Nohra, at the time, it was girl trouble.

"I was having problems with my girlfriend and somehow Coach Tressel found out," Nohra said. "We were in the process of breaking up and it caused me a lot of trauma in my first year at YSU. I was upset and Coach Tressel had a way of getting you to open up. I broke down into tears several times in front of Coach. He said to me, 'Joe, one day you're going to want to find a girl that you're going to treat like your mother. And when you talk and deal with your mother, you should treat her as special as you treat your girlfriend.'

"He was a big, big family guy," Nohra continued. "He always talked about his mom and dad, and when it came to the team, he always preached that we had to be a family and that we were all brothers and the coaching staff was part of the family and he was the father of our big family. I think that's why he's achieved so much success in life. For any coach that goes into sports, my advice is that you treat your team like a family and you get your kids to respect you and respect that family. It's going to breed success."

Nohra's story at Youngstown State, and all the other similar stories Tressel encountered and experienced with his players on and off the field, are why he probably would never leave the collegiate ranks.

"Coaching college football is like being in paradise," Tressel said. "You have great kids. They are at a time in their life when they are really growing. And there is no question, it would be hard to imagine anything better than this."

19 The Legacy of *The Winner's Manual*

When Tressel got the job at YSU in 1986, he endeavored to put together some kind of reference book that he could distribute to his players. He envisioned it as a guide to being a winner not just on the field, but also in life, and long after the players' football days were over. The result is a remarkable and wholly unique 300-plus page book called simply *The Winner's Manual*.

Tressel gives it out at the beginning of preseason camp each year along with the team playbook. Some consider it a playbook for life. Filled with inspirational quotes, anecdotes, short stories, and scriptures, among other things, its purpose is to inspire, inform, and guide its readers.

Former Buckeyes All-Big Ten wide receiver Anthony Gonzalez said the first time he saw *The Winner's Manual*, he noticed how big it was. Then he noticed how different it was. "I actually thought it was my playbook the first time I got it," he said. "Once I started looking at it, I just connected with so many of the different philosophies, especially as a freshman. You're going through some pretty difficult situations. You're away from home for the first time and you're not familiar with your surroundings and the people. I remember looking through the 'Handling Adversity' section daily because of how difficult that freshman transition was for me."

In the "Team" section of *The Winner's Manual*, there is a poem written by former Buckeyes safety Nate Salley. Salley was one of the hardest-hitting defensive backs in the Big Ten his senior season and was a fourth-round pick of the Carolina Panthers in the 2006

NFL draft. But before Salley, who loved to write poetry, ever played one down for Ohio State, he wrote a poem to his teammates at St. Thomas Aquinas High School in Fort Lauderdale just before graduation. Tressel was so moved by the poem that he has included it in *The Winner's Manual* every year.

WHAT YOU MEAN TO ME

What you mean to me,
Words can't even explain,
Just know without you,
My life would not be the same.

I'm going to miss you all,
When we go our separate ways,
I'd never thought I'd say this,
But I'm going to miss two-a-days.

The hard work was fun,
For it brought out the very best,
And when it came to competing,
We were better than the rest.

We never gave up,
We always played with heart,
We made up with hustle,
Whenever we didn't play smart.

Our coaches were a little tough,
But it always made us better,
And more important than ever,
It brought us all together.

So as we look towards the future,
I can assure you of one thing,

We may not always play with each other,
But, WE WILL ALWAYS BE A TEAM.

THANKS FOR EVERYTHING

Nate Salley, #21, Class of 2002

"I actually gave that poem to Coach [Bill] Conley when I was being recruited by Ohio State.... He gave it Coach Tressel, and Coach Tressel liked it—actually, Coach Tressel loved it," Salley recalled.

When Salley reported for preseason camp in August of his freshman year, *The Winner's Manual* for that year had already been printed and ready for distribution to players. But the following year, during a preseason meeting, Tressel distributed the newest *Winner's Manual* told all the players to turn to page 297. On that page was Salley's poem. Then, Tressel summoned Salley to the front of the room and had him read it to his teammates and the coaching staff. He asked Salley to stand in front of the team and read his poem every year he was at OSU.

NATE SALLEY

Position: Safety

Hometown: Fort Lauderdale, Florida

Years Played: 2002–2005

Career Highlights: Salley was one of the hardest hitters in the Big Ten. He was named a second-team All–Big Ten performer his sophomore season and a first-team all-conference selection in his junior season. During his senior year, Salley won Ohio State's Bo Rein Award, given to the team's most inspirational player.

"I loved that," Salley said about the opportunity to actually do a reading of his own poetry. "I really, really loved and appreciated that Coach Tressel let me do that. Knowing that my poem will always be there in *The Winner's Manual* is something very, very special to me. That was a great honor, even to this day as an NFL player. What I love about *The Winner's Manual* is that no matter what you're going through, there's always something in there for you."

"When Nate was making his adjustment from being away from home, because he was one of our Florida guys, he reflected on things like that," Tressel remembered. "He always liked to express himself with his poetry…. Poets have something about them that they write with that emotion and how they are feeling and they can put it into beautiful words. Nate had that talent."

Tressel probably never thought *The Winner's Manual* would help inspire a co-ed recreation softball team in Phoenix, Arizona. But former YSU wide receiver Ron "Bosco" Pearson introduced it to his team.

"I play third base on my co-ed softball team that I started here in Phoenix," Pearson said. "I can't play softball to save my life and every time a ball was hit to me, I ran the other way. Thank goodness this girl named Lindsay, who is a great athlete, was playing left field because she would clean up all of my mistakes. One particular year, we started the season 5–0. Then we must've started getting full of ourselves or something because we started to go downhill. So one day before a game, I actually took my *Winner's Manual* to the softball field and brought it into the dugout. Now, we're talking about a recreational softball league made up of men and women and here I am bringing Coach Tressel's *Winner's Manual* to the game so that we could all come together as a team. They got it and we got back on the winning track."

Butch Reynolds was named the speed coordinator for the Buckeyes football program in 2005. Reynolds, a former Ohio State track All-American, was hired by Tressel because the coach knew how important it was for his teams to be fast, and Reynolds was the man for the job. Reynolds set the world record in the 400-meter dash in 1988 with a time of 43.29. He won the Gold Medal in the 1988 Olympics in the 1,600-meter relay and the silver medal in the 400 meter individual races.

Reynolds said in all the years he was a competitive athlete, he had never seen anything like Tressel's *Winner's Manual*. "To me, if I was a football player at the Ohio State University, there would be two books that would be very important to me: one is the Bible, the other would be *The Winner's Manual*. Those are the only two books that would mean anything to me. It takes a special knowledge to understand your spiritual growth. You need a hunger for knowledge to really take advantage of the Bible and *The Winner's Manual*."

It was only natural that coaches who grew under Tressel's system and went on to secure head coaching positions of their own borrowed *The Winner's Manual* concept and implemented the same philosophies and principles in their own programs. Its success spoke for itself.

Mark Mangino, a Youngstown State graduate who had coached under Tressel at YSU and Ohio State, was named the Kansas Jayhawks head coach in 2002. Mangino has a *Victory Handbook* that he gives out to his players during preseason camp. "If you have principles that you believe in to help develop young men as players, as athletes, and as productive members of society, and you don't deviate from it and the kids know you believe in it, then they start to believe in it, then you'll develop successful men who will always work to be successful in every facet of their lives," said Mangino. In 2007, he led Kansas to one of its most successful seasons.

"One of the things that jumped out at me that Jim really believed in was how the whole *Winner's Manual* concept was about what he called the 'Wheel of Life' at YSU. Then, when we went to Ohio State, it was called the 'Block O of Life.' Whether you're a player or coach, if you live by the components of the Wheel of Life or Block O of Life, you have a chance to be successful and live a full life, even outside of football.

"Just because it's on a piece of paper doesn't mean that it's going to impact lives. The head coach has to live it and show it himself.

He has to be an example of the Wheel of Life that Jim has put together, and Jim has done that. Jim has worked hard in all areas of his life, his relationship with people, his faith, his work ethic, and all of those things and I think that's what really influences the players," Mangino said.

Jon Heacock, Tressel's top assistant at Youngstown State, took over the job when Tressel left for Ohio State in 2001, and he has kept the Youngstown State program thriving. In 2005 and 2006, the Penguins won the Gateway Football Conference championship. In 2006, they were a game away from playing in the Division I-AA national championship. Heacock was named the Gateway's Bruce Craddock Coach of the Year for the second straight year as well as the American Football Coaches Association's Division I-AA Region Four Coach of the Year and a finalist for the Eddie Robinson Award. His brother is Ohio State offensive coordinator Jim Heacock.

Jon Heacock said *The Winner's Manual* helped him and the program get through periods of adversity. "When I came back here to YSU after being fired from Indiana (where he was an assistant coach), Bill Knecht was on the YSU Board of Trustees and he was a really positive guy," Heacock said. "At some point, he got cancer.... The slogan that year in *The Winner's Manual* with Coach Tressel was 'Focus on the Moment,' and Coach Tressel had T-shirts and sweatshirts made with that slogan on them. Then, he had Bill come back later and he spoke to our team about his personal battle with cancer and what the whole *Winner's Manual* had done for him, because Coach Tressel had dropped it off at his house. I remember that being the rallying cry that whole year. [He was] a guy on the outside world who got a *Winner's Manual* and adopted the principles inside [it]," Heacock said. "He lived by it and was focusing on every single moment before he passed away in 2004."

Heacock said that if he had a coach leaving his program today, he guarantees one of the first things that coach would ask is if he could share *The Winner's Manual* with his new team. "I know if I ever left here, I'd pack up just one thing, and that would be *The Winner's Manual*," Heacock said.

Even if you weren't a coach or a player under Tressel, if you were directly around the program, you couldn't help but be inspired by *The Winner's Manual*. Joe Cassese, a longtime Youngstown State manager and son of Carmen Cassese, one of Tressel's closest friends, said there was a quote in *The Winner's Manual* that impacted him profoundly: "There will be 1,000 opportunities in your lifetime to keep your mouth shut. Take advantage of every one of them."

Joe Cassese was selling sporting goods full-time in Youngstown when he got a call from former YSU kicker Jeff Wilkins. Wilkins had been with the St. Louis Rams for a number of years and had played in two Super Bowls with them. He told Cassese that there was an opening in the Rams' equipment room, and that if Cassese was interested, he should send a resume and application. Getting the job was a pipe dream but he sent his resume anyway. Two weeks later, Cassese was at the family restaurant MVR when he received a call from Todd Hewitt, the equipment manager for the Rams. His father had been the Rams' equipment manager for 40 years before him. Todd Hewitt was just like Cassese, he had learned about hard work from his father. Cassese flew out to St. Louis three days later, and at the end of the day he had a job offer to work for the Rams.

The job was grueling, especially during training camp when the locker room could be open for 21 hours a day. Cassese would be in at 5 in the morning and stay past midnight. "Todd was a unique man, a guy who teaches lessons through examples, not a man of many words, but he was legendary in his trade," Cassese said. "He's the kind of guy who would throw something right back at you until you did it right.... I would ask questions and Todd didn't want questions, he wanted you to learn from the beginning. He'd show it to

you once and didn't want you to come back in and bother him....
It was a brutal situation in that there wasn't any compassion. You
knew you were either going to make it there and get it done or you
weren't."

There were hundreds, even thousands of times in the beginning
of Cassese's first three months in St. Louis when he wanted to fight
Hewitt, literally, or at least tell him how he really felt. Cassese didn't
know how much he could take. "Every time I got fed up with the fact
that I was working my butt off and this guy didn't seem like he was
appreciating it, I wanted to fight him," Cassese said.

"So many times I wanted to open my mouth and say, 'Look, how
about backing off a little bit?' But I just kept thinking about that quote
in *The Winner's Manual*. And I thought about my dad. And I thought
about Coach Tressel, and him saying 'There are a thousand opportunities in your lifetime to keep your mouth shut.' I was the low man
on the totem pole in St. Louis, the new guy in the NFL, and I never
opened my mouth."

Soon, Hewitt saw Cassese was a hard worker. Things got better
for Cassese and his relationship with Hewitt got progressively better, to the point that there was a level of mutual respect. "I'm great
friends with Todd now and I always will be because I'll never forget what he did for me in St. Louis," Cassese said. "I learned from a
legend."

Cassese later left St. Louis to take a similar job with the Cleveland
Browns. He was reluctant to leave Hewitt and the Rams but he
wanted the opportunity to get back closer to home. "Being in St.
Louis was a unique experience," he said. "But it could've been worse
had I not kept my mouth shut and not thought about Coach Tressel
and those words he preached in *The Winner's Manual*."

Tony Manna is one of those "outsiders" who had the privilege
of having *The Winner's Manual* in his possession for a period of time.
Manna, a 1983 Ohio State graduate from Akron, is a very successful

attorney and businessman. He is chairman of Signet Enterprises, LLC, a real estate development company, among other enterprises.

"I've never met Coach Tressel but as a proud Ohio State alum, I happened to look through *The Winner's Manual* [of] a friend, and it completely impressed me," Manna said. "Of all the things, [the one] that stood out to me was a story told by Sen. John McCain."

The story is about a young man from Alabama whom McCain met in captivity as prisoners of war in Vietnam. The prisoners occasionally would get care packages from their families delivered by the Red Cross; this young man's family was so poor that the only thing they could send him was a needle and thread. And the young man took that needle and thread and sewed an American flag on the inside of his shirt.

The prisoners tried to keep this a secret, but he was found out. The Vietnamese soldiers took him outside and beat him in front of the other prisoners to send a message. They threw him back in the mass cell bloodied and bruised, eyes almost closed shut from the beating, and barely able to move. The story continues that later that night, Sen. McCain looked over and saw the young man with the needle and thread in his hands, sewing another American flag to his shirt.

"To me, that says an awful lot and I tell that story all the time," Manna said. "When I talk to employees that are managers, I use it in two ways. I explain to them that we should be thankful for what we have in this country. I also use it in another context, to show inspiration, loyalty, and what that means to an organization. That young man kept those prisoners together. They saw that no obstacle was going to stop him from his belief, and when you've got that type of inspiration, that type of belief, that type of loyalty, organizations go very, very far."

Former Tressel players told stories about the impact *The Winner's Manual* had on their lives on and off the field:

Lorenzo Davis
YSU Running Back, 1986-1989

Davis was one of the players at Youngstown State who laid the ground-work in the early Tressel years for the Penguins' future success. He was a talented back and was a fast and strong runner, but Tressel moved him receiver in his senior year, where he excelled. Davis later played with the Pittsburgh Steelers.

Davis on "Team":

"My first impression of *The Winner's Manual* was, *How does this pertain to football?* It messed my mind up to try to figure out how this related to football. A perfect example of that is a play we used to run called 21. You really had to believe in your teammates to run that play. It was a running play run between the tackle and a tight end. You can run that play three or four times, and you might only get one yard, and you want to go to the outside or cut it inside before you're supposed to. But Coach Tressel would keep saying, 'It will open up. Believe in your teammates. Believe that the hole will open up.' Then, all of a sudden, that fifth time you run it, it's wide open, and you pop it for a 55-yard touchdown run. That's when you understand what it's like to keep believing in your teammates.

"I tell my students and players that you never quit—ever—no matter how down you feel, how bad you're losing, no matter what.

LORENZO DAVIS

Position: Running Back

Hometown: Fort Lauderdale, Florida

Years Played: 1986-1989

Career Highlights: Davis, a YSU Hall of Fame inductee, started out as a running back but was later moved to a slotback/wide receiver by Tressel his senior year. He ended his career with 122 career receptions, fifth on the school's all-time list. He is the only player in YSU football history to amass 1,000 yards rushing and 1,000 yards in receiving.

My middle school basketball team here in Broward County [Florida] hasn't lost a game in three years. We'll practice hard, and at the end of practice we shoot free throws. I'll set up a scenario where we're I tell them we're down by one or two points. I'll put everybody on the baseline and ask who wants to shoot the free throw. Guys will start yelling, 'Me! Me! Me!' I'll put in the guy who tries to hide or won't say anything. I want him to believe he can make it. I want his teammates to believe he's going to make it.

"That's what I relay to my guys: everything about 'team' that's in *The Winner's Manual*. You have to believe in each other. You have to believe that the man next to you is going to handle his responsibility. It got to the point where, during the season, we didn't care who was going to shoot the free throws, we believed in him. We believed in everybody on the team. We believe in everybody today.

"One of the things that we started my senior year at YSU...[was] the 'beehive.' It was a thing [we did] when, before a game, at halftime, and after a game, we would all get as close as we could to one another and we would go onto the field really slowly, taking small steps. We were so close together, it was like the bees swarming out of a beehive in one big mass. The beehive is all about believing in one another as a team. We came on the field together and we left the field together, regardless of the outcome.... That beehive took us a long way. And you know what? Ohio State uses the beehive to this day."

Davis on "Work":

"I always hear people talk about Youngstown State, and even Ohio State, being lucky when we would win close games.... It wasn't luck. We worked harder than anyone else. The way we conditioned at the end of every practice helped put us in a position to win games at the end.

"We would run sprints at the end of every practice and Coach Tressel would tell everybody to put their hands on the line. If just

Players at Youngstown State created the "beehive," a ritual of entering and exiting the football field in a tight cluster, to underscore team unity and togetherness.

one person didn't have their hand on the line, he wouldn't say anything. He'd wait until we ran the sprint then he'd tell us to get back on the line. And believe me, that happened a lot. Even when you know to put your hand on the line, when you're tired, that's when most people lose their concentration. They know what they are supposed to do but they are too tired and their body just won't let them do something the right way. You want to take the shortcut or sell yourself short. *The Winner's Manual* taught you not to do that.... Coach Tressel taught you not to do that....

"We were conditioned enough so that at the end of a game, no one was ready to quit. Everybody had it in their mind that they had to do their jobs and work hard at it. If a lineman had to take two steps to the right to make a block, he didn't take one because he was tired, he took two steps."

Davis on "Humility":
"Reading through *The Winner's Manual* and watching Coach Tressel apply those principles, you learn to become humble and patient with others—just because of the way Coach Tressel handles his program. If you make a mistake, he's always going to give you a chance to redeem yourself. That redemption and humility to me is what helped Ohio State win the national championship against Miami in 2002. Ohio State had a great team that year, but at the end of the game, they had a chance to redeem themselves and they did.

"Miami was called for a pass interference in overtime on fourth down...and Ohio State got another chance to redeem themselves—and they scored. But that wasn't the game-winning touchdown, because Miami got the ball back and still got another chance—a chance to redeem themselves—and they didn't.... They let that one call hold them back. The bottom line was Miami didn't finish the task at hand."

A.J. Hawk
Ohio State Linebacker, 2002–2005

A.J. Hawk on *The Winner's Manual*:
"When some guys come in when they are freshmen and see *The Winner's Manual*, maybe the first couple days or first week they don't take it really seriously and they might think, *What are we doing here, why are we writing down a diary every day during preseason camp?*

"The first thing [we did] when we met as a team in the morning during camp is turn to the back of *The Winner's Manual* [to] a section called 'Quiet Time.' Every day, we had to write down what we were thankful for.... Three days into that, I really started to enjoy it, and I really loved those 10 or 15 minutes we'd have every morning when we'd go through the different sections.

"Everyone is connected to each other through that *Winner's Manual*, whether you went to Youngstown State or Ohio State. We may not have ever met each other, but we're all connected."

Hawk on "Heroes/Winners":

"There is a nice story about Pat Tillman in the 'Heroes/Winners' section that really means a lot to me. With everything that Pat Tillman stood for and believed in before he was killed tragically in Afghanistan, I just had so much respect for him and his family. I love his attitude and character, and I never knew him personally. I've talked to people who knew him and I really respect that he stood his ground, did his stuff his way, and said, 'I don't care what everyone else thinks me.' He left a lot of money on the table when he left the NFL to enlist in the service and fight in Afghanistan. It seemed like his whole life he did things differently, or did things that didn't really conform to the norms of everyday life. I think everyone wishes they could be a little bit more like that, and I think that's what I respected about him."

Simon Fraser
Ohio State Defensive Lineman, 2001-2004

Fraser was an exceptional player at Ohio State, and he epitomized the term "student-athlete." He was instrumental in the Buckeyes' 2002 national championship. More impressively, he was a three-time scholar-athlete at Ohio State who earned academic All-Big Ten Conference honors twice. Fraser has played three seasons with the Cleveland Browns and one with the Atlanta Falcons.

"There are 19 different components in *The Winner's Manual* and when you actually think about it, they're all intertwined. In every game I encountered, I experienced several of [them]. And I don't think

The Winner's Manual has the same impact on you the first year as it does the second year. I remember our sophomore year Coach Tressel was talking to us and mentioned that LeCharles Bentley, who was a second-round pick for the New Orleans Saints, had called up and asked Coach Tressel for a *Winner's Manual* for his training camp.... That's how important *The Winner's Manual* was to LeCharles, and how much it means to all of us."

LeCharles Bentley
Ohio State Offensive Lineman, 1998–2001

Bentley on "Toughness":

"When I first saw *The Winner's Manual*, I thought it was actually really silly. I didn't see the point of it. Once I actually opened it up and allowed myself to be open to it, I understood the point of it, and how it could really help you with more than just the aspect of being a better a football player. I was able to apply different things in it to life. That's what I really liked about it—it wasn't a playbook. A playbook is designed to just help you become a better player.... *The Winner's Manual* is like your playbook for life, and that's how Coach Tressel was able to convince a lot of people to buy into it. I've been gone from Ohio State for several years but I still like to get *The Winner's Manual* every year....

"There is one quote...that has always stuck with me: 'When you're going through hell, keep going.' It's a simple quote, but it means so much to me. It means no matter how hard things are getting or no matter how bad things look, you have to keep going, because you can't just stay where [you] are. You have to pick yourself up and keep moving forward. No matter who you are, there is always somebody that has gone through what you have gone through, and you just have to fight your way through any of the tough battles and struggles that you may face."

Kirk Barton
Ohio State Offensive Tackle, 2004–2007

Barton was one of the more vocal players on the team, as well as one of the steadiest linemen in the school's history. A senior co-captain, he finished the season with a unique distinction.

Barton on "Focus":

"After we lost to Illinois [in 2007], our focus wasn't 'Aw man, we lost our first game of the season.' Our focus was on just bouncing back the next week because it was Michigan Week. At about 10:00 that night of the Illinois loss, I started watching film on Michigan. There was nothing else we could do about the Illinois loss, but we still had a big challenge ahead of us…. Guys were starting to worry about bowl games, rankings, and booking their travel plans, and I felt we needed to get focused on Michigan—and that's what we all did. We knew we had to handle our business.

"And once we did, we had intense practices all week, and we beat Michigan 14–3 at the Big House. I later found out that I am the only Buckeye to beat Michigan four years as a starter and I think the only player from either team…. I never thought about that when I first got to Ohio State. My focus was just playing the best I could every game of my career—especially against Michigan."

Dimitrios Makridis
Ohio State Long Snapper, 2005–2007

Makridis, the son of first-generation Greek immigrants, lived his life in accordance with the principles of The Winner's Manual. *They were values instilled in him long before Ohio State, values taught by his parents. Makridis demonstrated that with hard work, faith, and belief in oneself, anything can be achieved.*

Makridis on "Excellence":

"The first thing I thought when I got *The Winner's Manual* as a freshman was that it is a manual of all the things my father has taught me my entire life....

"The 'Excellence' section of *The Winner's Manual* is what I loved the most, and I always look through it during the season and even after the season. There's one part of it that stays with me all the time, and it says:

"Whoever said 'It's not whether you win or lose that counts,' probably lost. There are winners and there are losers. And if you choose to be one of the former, the journey through life can be a little lonely.

"When you're a winner, you have to set the standard for excellence wherever you go. You have to battle against fatigue, the intimidation, the human tendency to just want to take things a little easier.

"You have to be able to come up with, time and

DIMITRIOS MAKRIDIS

Position: Long Snapper

Hometown: Warren, Ohio

Years Played: 2005–2007

Career Highlights: Makridis showed persistence during his career at Ohio State, starting as a walk-on linebacker and becoming the starting long snapper for the Buckeyes. He attended the same high school as Ohio State running back Maurice Clarett and Ohio State great and Pro Football Hall of Fame wide receiver Paul Warfield.

time again, one consistently great performance after another.'

"Honestly, that's a reminder of how I've always lived my life. When I was in high school, my friends would go and do something completely different from what I wanted to do, and I'd make up some excuse why I couldn't go along with them because I had a higher priority, in my honest opinion.... I did my own thing. I went to the weight room. I worked out. I went home and just stayed with my family. The peer pressure in high school didn't bother me at all because I was striving for excellence in every phase of my life. It sucked sometimes because I knew I could be out with my friends, but I knew in the end, all of my hard work and sacrifice would pay off."

Makridis on "Persistence":
"I came to Ohio State hoping to be a linebacker because I was a linebacker in high school. When I walked on, they listed me as a long snapper, but in my mind I felt like I was a linebacker. I had played my entire first year as a linebacker on scout team.

"Until one day, one of the coaching staff said, 'Look, you're a long snapper and you need to work on that.' When that happened, it completely changed everything. You just practice one thing: snapping the ball. You're focusing on just one thing and it's what you do. You master that technique to the point that you're not even thinking about it anymore. Even though now, as a long snapper, you're only playing about 10 downs a game, there's still a lot more pressure on you because of what you do.

"From the beginning, when I first got here, I wasn't used to the system. It was a much bigger school. In high school, everyone knows you, everyone says hi. Here, you come in and not too many people talk to you. You're kind of like a number. You do your own thing. If you don't take care of yourself, nobody is going to help you out.

"That was probably the hardest thing for me.... Without persistence, there's no way you can make it through that. But I understood that I had to wait and be patient because here at The Ohio State University, you're expected to win. So part of that waiting is learning the whole process and taking in that entire experience. Now, I have my shot. And because the coaching staff and my teammates make you so mentally prepared, when I get to this point, I know it's time for me to step up and show what I've got, and I feel confident."

Makridis on "Attitude":

"When the coaching staff moved me from linebacker to long snapper, my attitude and mentality was, *Don't complain. You'll get through it somehow.* And it's what my dad taught me: the worst thing that somebody can do is find an excuse. Then they have a reason as to why they didn't do something."

Makridis on "Toughness":

"I would categorize the 2007 team as a tough team and, in my opinion, it was the toughest team I've seen since I've been here. And it wasn't even certain games that made us a tough team, it was the way that we prepared and the attitude that we had. We just worked so hard and we had the mentality that there's no team that could have worked as hard as we did. Even though we had a disappointing loss against Florida in the national championship, I think we worked harder than anyone in the country."

Dick Tressel
Ohio State Running Backs Coach

Dick, Jim's older brother, first came to Ohio State as the associate director of football operations and now is the running backs coach. Tressel had a 124-102-2 record over 23 seasons as head coach of Hamline University in St. Paul, Minnesota.

Dick Tressel on "Focus":

"I was aware of *The Winner's Manual*...but I really didn't start looking at it [regularly] until I joined Jim here at Ohio State. That's when the process of learning and reading *The Winner's Manual* started to become really beneficial to me, the focus you need to get things done every day in your life.

"As a team, we always start the morning together with a quiet period at the beginning of the day. [There is] one part that always works for me. It's a quote that reads, 'The first hour is the rudder of the day.' That's what jumps out to me. The great thing about it is that no one who reads *The Winner's Manual* has the same definition of what it means to them; it has different meanings for everyone."

Damion Matthews
Youngstown State Wide Receiver, 1998–1999

Matthews was a transfer from Indiana University in the Big Ten, but his biggest moment as a Penguin was in 1999 when he caught a 10-yard touchdown pass with 44 seconds left to help give YSU a 27–24 win against Florida A&M and a berth in the national championship game against Georgia Southern.

Matthews on "Team":

"The way Coach Tressel brought us together as a team, and what he did for our senior class, was something that helped build me into who I am today, no question. He got us to believe in each other and trust one another…. My senior year, we made it to the national championship game—but during the course of the regular season, we were down at least three games 21–0 at halftime or somewhere in the third quarter, and we believed. Each play, you have some teammates who see something on the field and once they do their assignment, they want to run over and help someone take care of their assignment, then they leave a gap open. It's a natural instinct, but that's not playing as a team. You have to trust that everyone will handle their own assignment and that's what we had, trust in each other. That was a big reason why we made it to the national championship in 1999."

Matthews on "Faith/Belief":

"It was easy for us to fight back during my senior season because we had the faith, belief, and work ethic so that we could always come back and win a game. There had to be two minutes left in the game and us down by 21 points for us to even think we may lose....

"When we played Florida A&M in the national semifinals in 1999, we were behind 24–13 at home. But Tim Johnson's interception turned the momentum of the game, and with just 44 seconds remaining.

"I can remember like it was yesterday. Florida A&M was on our 12-yard line leading by 11 points, and we called a timeout. Kawonza Swan and Tim Johnson [had] watched film all week. They knew when Florida A&M got in the red zone, they liked to throw the slant. So during the time out, Kawonza went to Tim and told him, 'Watch out for the slant. It's coming.'

"It goes back to the trust and belief. Tim listened to Kawonza and Florida A&M called the slant. Tim stepped in, picked the ball off, and returned into Florida A&M's territory. The momentum from that play shifted in our favor, and a few plays later, Elliott Giles went in and scored. Then, Florida A&M got the ball back after the kickoff, we held them and with 44 seconds left, and I scored the game-winning touchdown on a 10-yard pass from Jeff Ryan. That game was all about having the belief that we were going to win and we never quit, never. That belief helped us make it to the national championship game."

Matthews on "Discipline":

"I learned so many things from Coach Tressel and *The Winner's Manual*, but one of the biggest things I learned is that when you're supposed to be somewhere at 4:00, 3:55 is on time, but it's actually late.... Don't be on time, because 'on time' is late. Coach Tressel is a very prompt person. He's always early.... He taught us that, and I carried that over into my job. If I have to be there at 8, I'm there at 7:30 or 7:45."

Tressel still has it as he poses in the drop-back position that he was accustomed to as a star quarterback for his dad, Lee Tressel, at Baldwin-Wallace College.

Matthews on "Work":

"When I first got to YSU in 1997, we ran a lot during our preseason conditioning, and even during the regular season. I don't think anybody in the country ran as many sprints and worked out as hard as we did. I think that was a big reason why we made it to the national championship that year; we beat McNeese State 10–9 in a defensive battle and a game that went down to the wire. We only had 200 total yards for the game and we were down 9-3 going into the fourth quarter.

"The great thing about Coach Tressel is that he listens to his players.... We would tell him what's going on and we would tell him what play to run and that next possession he would actually run that play. Because of that, the players trust him just as much as he trusts us. In my opinion, that's what makes him a great coach."

Ray Isaac
Youngstown State Quarterback, 1988–1991
Isaac was one of those local boys who stayed home to play for Tressel. One of Youngstown State's all-time gifted athletes, he was the starting quarterback when the Penguins won their first Division I-AA national championship in 1991.

Isaac on *The Winner's Manual*:
"When we came in for one of the [preseason] meetings…we already knew what we had to do; *The Winner's Manual* spelled it all out for us. It also showed who was not really for the team and who was not buying into the philosophies…who was and wasn't going to deviate from the process of being a winner.

"I remember Coach Tressel telling me, 'Ray, if you get a piece *The Winner's Manual* inside you, it's going to be hard for you to let it go.'"

Steve Jones
Youngstown State Fullback, 1986–1989

A player on Tressel's first Youngstown State team in 1986, Jones has maintained a close relationship with his former coach.

Jones on "Responsibility/Do Right":

"If we didn't perform at the level that we thought we should, or that the coaching staff thought we should, Coach Tressel would always talk about us doing a self-assessment on what we could've done differently...that may have had a different impact on the game.... When we didn't do well—or even after games where we did play well and won—we never reached perfection, so we knew we still had a lot of work ahead of us....

"When I talk to my former teammates who played for Coach Tressel, we always talk about the accomplishments that we have made in the private sector or in business, and we always refer back to...the principles and philosophies Coach Tressel instilled in us."

———

Jack Park, a noted Ohio State football historian, couldn't help but compare Tressel's coaching style, the way he led his players on and off the field, to the legendary Green Bay Packers coach Vince Lombardi. Lombardi led his team to a level of success very few coaches ever achieve. In 1959, he inherited a team that had won only one game in its previous season, a season that included an embarrassing 56–0 loss to the Baltimore Colts. In fact, the Packers had not posted a winning record in their last 11 seasons. But using virtually the same players from the 1958 team, Lombardi guided them to a winning mark of 7–5 in 1959, an appearance in the NFL title game in 1960, and victories in the next two NFL championships with wins over the New York Giants in 1961 and 1962.

In Lombardi's last seven seasons in Green Bay, the Packers won five NFL titles, including victories over the Kansas City Chiefs (35–10) and Oakland Raiders (33–14) in the first two Super Bowls.

"In his own way, Vince Lombardi lived many of the '19 Fundamentals for Winners' that are part of Coach Jim Tressel's *Winner's Manual*," Park said. "Lombardi's players quickly realized how much he truly cared for them as individuals. He brought a much-needed discipline to the entire organization, an attribute that had been noticeably absent.

"His son, Vince Lombardi, Jr., once stated that the three things that were important to his father were God, his family, and the Green Bay Packers—in that order," Park said. "Tressel is the same way, regardless of the level he is coaching."

Jim Tressel publicly spoke about why *The Winner's Manual* is such an important tool for him as it relates to the development of his players. He writes about it in great detail in his successful book, *The Winner's Manual*.

For this book, Tressel has given a brief statement on the personal significance of each of the 19 fundamentals of *The Winner's Manual*:

On Attitude: "At every moment in time, our attitude is the one thing that we can always control. Our attitude is truly our most powerful tool."

On Caring: "At the end of it all, our greatest legacy is how much we truly cared about others. The team. The school. The community. The state. The fans. The nation. The world. Our creator."

On Class: "Without class, all accomplishments are irrelevant."

On Discipline: "If consistency is the hallmark of greatness, then discipline must abound."

On Enthusiasm: "A person with endless enthusiasm and endless spirit will excel."

On Excellence: "The dogged pursuit of excellence is deserved in all phases of life."

On Faith/Belief: "Every achiever has it, every championship team portrays it."

On Focus: "In this highly competitive, intensely busy world in which we exist, the secret is to be able to focus on the moment."

On Gratitude: "The only way to have proper perspective is to be genuinely grateful for God's many blessings and opportunities."

On Handling Adversity/Handling Success: "While handling adversity requires great faith and toughness, handling success is the most difficult challenge."

On Heroes/Winners: "Life is too short to learn everything we need on our own. We must choose those we believe in as winners and heroes very carefully."

On Hope: "If we have hope, that is all we need. We just need a chance."

On Humility: "Humility helps us understand that the world does not revolve around us, but we are simply a small part of God's master plan."

On Love: "Love encompasses all good things for the well-being of others."

On Persistence: "The road is too long and the mountain too steep to be traveled without extraordinary persistence."

On Responsibility/Doing Right: "Without constant attention to doing our part and doing it right, we cannot be a positive part of the whole, whether that whole is a family, team, school, church, community, or a civilization."

On Team: "Football is so popular because it truly teaches that all members are important."

On Toughness: "Mental or physical, the true champions in life possess the toughness to handle all that comes their way."

On Work: "British actor Sir Noel Coward stated that 'Work is much more fun than fun.' When you have that feeling, you have found your perfect life's work."

Afterword
Tom Cousineau: An Open Letter from a Buckeye Great

Tom Cousineau was an All-American linebacker for Ohio State from 1975 to 1978. He played for the legendary Coach Woody Hayes and in addition to being his last team captain was also Hayes' last in a great line of All-Americans.

During his illustrious collegiate career, Cousineau was a three-time All-Big Ten selection, named an All-American twice, and won the Big Ten Conference MVP award. He still holds most of the tackling records at Ohio State, including most tackles in a game (29 vs. Penn State, 1978) and most tackles in a season (211, in 1978).

Cousineau was the No. 1 overall player selected in the 1979 NFL draft by Buffalo and, dating back to 1936, was the only Ohio State player in the history of the draft to be selected No. 1 overall. Since then, two other former Buckeyes were selected No. 1 overall in the draft, Dan Wilkinson (1994, Cincinnati) and Orlando Pace (1997, St. Louis).

But Cousineau turned down Buffalo's offer and instead played for the Montreal Alouettes in the CFL, where he was All-CFL 1979-1981 and MVP of the Grey Cup (Canada's version of the Super Bowl) in 1980. He then signed a free agent contract with the Cleveland Browns in 1982 and played for them for four years, earning All-NFL honors in 1983 and 1984. Cousineau later played two seasons with the San Francisco 49ers (1986–1987) before retiring from football.

Though he never played for Tressel, the two have built a solid friendship over the years. Cousineau offered this open letter about what Tressel's coaching philosophies and his philosophies about life mean to him.

I love the way the first line reads, "It's not about you," in the mega-successful book, *The Purpose Driven Life*. Next to The Bible, it is one of the most-read books. This line is the author's premise and starting point as he attempts to help us answer the question, "Why am I here and for what purpose do I exist?" I believe the "what's in it for me"-isms of our day have reached their perfectly illogical selfish conclusions. Our obsession with self is destroying our ability to rightly deal with the tough situations and hard decisions we face daily, and in asking why and how.

Coach is a role that contemplates so much more than wins and losses. Coaches are in a unique position to influence, mentor, and mold America's student-athletes, people who invest enormous amounts of time, energy, and emotion into their teams. Like Woody Hayes, a man I was so honored to play for, Jim Tressel isn't so much about players as he is about people and helping them to express their God-given talents both on and off the football field.

As you listen to his players' stories, you know Coach Tressel is not afraid to talk about and drill down into the whys and hows of living, training, and competing honorably while teaching his young men how to connect with and sacrifice for others in the pursuit of something bigger and more important than themselves.

The caring attitude Coach Tressel has for people, in my opinion, comes from being raised by two terrific parents, Eloise and Lee Tressel. I have a number of friends who played for Lee Tressel at Baldwin-Wallace College and they hold him in great, almost mythical, regard. I remember being at the press conference in Columbus when Coach Tressel was named the head coach of Ohio State. I had met Mrs. Tressel years before at an awards banquet when I was in high school. Although many years had passed, Mrs. Tressel came up to me that day and said hello. Not only did she remember my name, but she asked about my dad, who had been a lifelong high school football coach. We had a wonderful conversation about football and many other things. To Mrs. Tressel, I was important, even on the day that her son was achieving a lifelong dream. That's where Coach Tressel gets it; it is wired into his DNA.

The players he has coached didn't care what Coach Tressel knew until they knew he cared about them first, which they found out quickly. One of the overwhelming examples of Coach Tressel's genuine concern for people is in his office. The coach's door is almost always open, and at the corner of his desk is a prayer request box. That is a man who cares about people. Whether you are a coach, a player, a manager, or whomever, he wants you to put something in that box that needs prayer.

But this is about more than Jim Tressel being a sincerely good person, because goodness and sincerity don't just happen. These important qualities that are so evident in both the coaching style and lifestyle of Coach Tressel are borne out of his pursuit of God's truths and wisdom.

Coach Tressel likes to quote Psalm 111, which states, "The beginning of wisdom is the fear of God." Coach Tressel has talked to me about the fact that we think we are pretty smart, that we think we know everything and can be everything, that we are Ohio State and that we are somehow special just because and that we can become great through experience and knowledge alone, but that if we don't acknowledge God as the creator and source of all things, then we will find ourselves on shaky ground and be prone to mistakes and foolish choices.

This view is an acknowledgement that it is a good thing to contemplate and dwell upon the works of God, not only in the world, but right here at The Ohio State University. It is about respect, fear, honor, and gratitude all rolled up into an attitude that witnesses the works of an active God and is the prerequisite starting point that allows us to pursue the development of wisdom in our lives. It is about the idea that there is something bigger in this world than our personal statistics or what others are telling us. It is about the things that reside in our hearts that can be actively demonstrated in our daily living.

These guys, a group of highly talented athletes, who come from all over the country and each with different backgrounds, different values, and different goals, are asked to form a unique brotherhood. Coach Tressel has these kids for three to four years, sometimes five, and at a time when they are really engaged and will listen to him. But listen, we are all selfish people, who always want to know, *What's in it for me? How can I get the playing time at the position I want with the publicity and the stats I've always dreamed about?* Coach Tressel and his staff are able to get these kids to focus on taking a closer look at what is underneath each and every one of them, and to slowly develop a character that reflects an earnest search for the truth and for the wisdom that will serve each of them not only on the football field, but for the many more years they will have as non-players.

Coach Tressel has never coached a perfect game; none of his players have ever played a perfect game. We are all works in progress. It is a process.

I had the great fortune to play for Coach Woody Hayes. He loved Ohio State desperately and always talked about "team first," and how the only way to win was with people. But Woody didn't talk so much about how you get there and how you do it. He just insisted that you do it. Conversation over! As a coach, you can stand up in front of a team and talk to them, but unless you require them to respond back to you, you won't get that deep connection with what's important and why.

When you talk about things like sacrifice, giving, and putting the team first, it is possible to do so without love for the team. But it is impossible to love the team without giving. If you have love, you will always give, and that is what every team should be after.

Like I said, it's a process. It doesn't happen overnight, and Coach Tressel doesn't expect that. Not all of these kids are successful and I'm not representing that. Coach Tressel is not trying to create a team of choirboys, because you can't win that way. He is trying to help develop good character and high-quality young men utilizing the inspiration and wisdom of so many before him. He is not attempting to do this alone. He has tapped into the philosophies of the legendary John Wooden (UCLA men's basketball coach), Confucius and Winston Churchill, to Jesus Christ. An incredible amount of time-tested wisdom and truths have gone into this collection of words to live by.

Let's say somebody who doesn't know anything about Ohio State, or isn't really a college football fan, runs into Coach Tressel and asks him what kind of team he thinks he is going to have. This question can be answered one of two ways. The first contemplates wins and losses, which is very important. Lofty goals are good and attainment of them is even better. However, the other answer is that you won't often know what kind of a team you will have until 30 years from now. After the process has had a good amount of time to germinate, after those players and that team have applied the values and things they learned from Coach Tressel into their personal and professional lives. Long after they have played, that's when we will know what kind of team we had.

I want to be a good father, a good brother, a good son. I want to be a good teammate, a good friend. But how do I do that? Players can understand what Coach Tressel is saying from an intellectual perspective. The truth is, though, that until it travels two feet south to the heart and resides in that place where they have made these truths and wisdom their own, they won't fully understand. That's why it's a process. Good things take time and are more prone to endure. The stories the players tell in this book testify to the fact that time spent with Jim Tressel where the rubber meets the road is where we know that this works. These are great stories of lives that have been impacted, even changed, of men who have gone on to be much more than football players.

Generally speaking, teams with better character are better teams. It doesn't happen by hanging a couple of slogans above the door or delivering a couple of heartfelt pregame speeches. If Coach Tressel's players can take what they've learned and plant it in their minds, and, more importantly, in their hearts, they will be able to deliver on a constant theme of the great coach Woody Hayes: that every Ohio State football player be equipped and committed not so much to paying it back as to paying it forward.

Coach Tressel walks this out with his players on a daily basis. The bad news is that there will be a test on all of this—in fact, there will be many. The good news is that you don't have to get a perfect score. Only one guy ever has.

Remember, it is a process.

YEA OHIO!

Acknowledgments

In the 20-plus years I've been a journalist, this is the most important piece of writing I've ever produced. It's easy to say that, because I am who I am because of Youngstown State University. I am who I am because of what I learned there, and the Tressel-YSU connection means so much to me.

I first have to thank Coach Tressel for listening to my idea, and then having the faith in me to allow me to do it. He always treated me as if I were the most important person in the world, like he did everyone else. He's an amazing person and a great motivator. Forget about sports. He cares about you as a person—who you are and what you can become in life.

Thanks to all of my friends at Youngstown State who, like me, had the privilege and pleasure of being at YSU in the mid-'80s when Coach Tressel took over the program and transformed it into a national powerhouse. And to all of the new Ohio State friends I met in the process of writing this book, thanks for enthusiastically wanting to be part of this project.

Dr. Bege Bowers, Dr. Sherry Linkon, Dr. Brady, and the rest of the YSU English Department have been amazing to me and all of them have shaped me as a writer.

Greg Gulas, my dear friend, you have always been one of my biggest supporters. I don't know many people with the sports knowledge you possess and the professionalism you display in everything you do. Thanks, my man.

Thanks to YSU sports information director Trevor Parks and his staff for access to photographs and whatever other YSU-related archives I needed for this project. It is greatly appreciated.

Lisa Solley, the managing editor at *The Warren-Tribune Chronicle*, a colleague and friend who was the first female sports reporter at the YSU school newspaper, *The Jambar*, to cover YSU football and Jim Tressel. Lisa is a sports junkie and the self-proclaimed "biggest Jim Tressel fan in the world." Thanks for your photos—and your support.

Thanks also to Gary Housteau of Bucknuts, a fellow Mahoning Valley guy who never hesitated to help when I asked for it. His Ohio State photos in this book help bring a personal touch to most of the stories.

Thanks to all of the former players, coaches, and acquaintances of Coach Tressel.

To my wife, Tricia, and children, Trey, Christian, Brooke, Cameron, and our dogs Vinnie and Edie, every gratitude for all of your love and support.

To Principal Adam Hill, Mrs. Harris, and all the teachers, students, and staff at Crestwood Middle School, thanks for making my character education program a success. You guys are *awesome*! And students, remember: keep your blinders on, stay disciplined, and don't ever, ever, waste a minute in school. You'll never get that time back. And someone give Craig Turner a pencil.

Donald and Walter, you guys are my inspiration.

And for my YSU family, here are some words that might bring back some memories:

The Brass Rail

The Pit and "sauce on fries"

C. Staples

Pal Joey's

New Music Station

The College Inn

Little Jimmy's

Like Edith and Archie sang, "Those Were the Days!"

Go 'Guins! Go Bucks!